W0115169

▶ **Network Society and Future Scenarios for a Collaborative Economy**

DOI: 10.1057/9781137406897.0001

Other Palgrave Pivot titles

Tom Watson (editor): Eastern European Perspectives on the Development of Public Relations: Other Voices

Erik Paul: Australia as US Client State: The Geopolitics of De-Democratization and Insecurity

Floyd Weatherspoon: African-American Males and the U.S. Justice System of Marginalization: A National Tragedy

Mark Axelrod: No Symbols Where None Intended: Literary Essays from Laclos to Beckett

Paul M. W. Hackett: Facet Theory and the Mapping Sentence: Evolving Philosophy, Use and Application

Irwin Wall: France Votes: The Election of François Hollande

David J. Staley: Brain, Mind and Internet: A Deep History and Future

Georgiy Voloshin: The European Union's Normative Power in Central Asia: Promoting Values and Defending Interests

Shane McCorristine: William Corder and the Red Barn Murder: Journeys of the Criminal Body

Catherine Blair: Securing Pension Provision: The Challenge of Reforming the Age of Entitlement

Zarlasht M. Razeq: UNDP's Engagement with the Private Sector, 1994–2011

James Martin: Drugs On the Dark Net: How Cryptomarkets Are Transforming the Global Trade in Illicit Drugs

Shin Yamashiro: American Sea Literature: Seascapes, Beach Narratives, and Underwater Explorations

Sudershan Goel, Barbara A. Sims, and Ravi Sodhi: Domestic Violence Laws in the United States and India: A Systematic Comparison of Backgrounds and Implications

Gregory Sandstrom: Human Extension: An Alternative to Evolutionism, Creationism and Intelligent Design

Kirsten Harley and Gary Wickham: Australian Sociology: Fragility, Survival, Rivalry

Eugene Halton: From the Axial Age to the Moral Revolution: John Stuart-Glennie, Karl Jaspers, and a New Understanding of the Idea

Joseph Kupfer: Meta-Narrative in the Movies: Tell Me a Story

Sami Pihlström: Taking Evil Seriously

Ben La Farge: The Logic of Wish and Fear: New Perspectives on Genres of Western Fiction

Samuel Taylor-Alexander: On Face Transplantation: Life and Ethics in Experimental Biomedicine

Graham Oppy: Reinventing Philosophy of Religion: An Opinionated Introduction

Ian I. Mitroff and Can M. Alpaslan: The Crisis-Prone Society: A Brief Guide to Managing the Beliefs That Drive Risk in Business

Takis S. Pappas: Populism and Crisis Politics in Greece

G. Douglas Atkins: T.S. Eliot and the Fulfillment of Christian Poetics

palgrave▶pivot

Network Society and Future Scenarios for a Collaborative Economy

▶

Vasilis Kostakis
Research Fellow, Tallinn University of Technology, Estonia

and

Michel Bauwens
Founder, P2P Foundation

palgrave
macmillan

DOI: 10.1057/9781137406897.0001

© Vasilis Kostakis and Michel Bauwens 2014

All rights reserved. No reproduction, copy or transmission of this publication may be made without written permission.

No portion of this publication may be reproduced, copied or transmitted save with written permission or in accordance with the provisions of the Copyright, Designs and Patents Act 1988, or under the terms of any licence permitting limited copying issued by the Copyright Licensing Agency, Saffron House, 6–10 Kirby Street, London EC1N 8TS.

Any person who does any unauthorized act in relation to this publication may be liable to criminal prosecution and civil claims for damages.

The authors have asserted their rights to be identified as the author of this work in accordance with the Copyright, Designs and Patents Act 1988.

First published 2014 by
PALGRAVE MACMILLAN

Palgrave Macmillan in the UK is an imprint of Macmillan Publishers Limited, registered in England, company number 785998, of Houndmills, Basingstoke, Hampshire RG21 6XS.

Palgrave Macmillan in the US is a division of St Martin's Press LLC, 175 Fifth Avenue, New York, NY 10010.

Palgrave Macmillan is the global academic imprint of the above companies and has companies and representatives throughout the world.

Palgrave® and Macmillan® are registered trademarks in the United States, the United Kingdom, Europe and other countries.

ISBN: 978–1–13740–688–0 EPUB
ISBN: 978–1–13740–689–7 PDF
ISBN: 978–1–13741–506–6 Hardback

A catalogue record for this book is available from the British Library.

A catalog record for this book is available from the Library of Congress.

www.palgrave.com/pivot

DOI: 10.1057/9781137406897

Contents

List of Figures

Preface

The aim of this book is not to provide yet another critique of capitalism but rather to contribute to the ongoing dialogue for post-capitalist construction, and to discuss how another world could be possible. We build on the idea that peer-to-peer infrastructures are gradually becoming the general conditions of work, economy and society, considering peer production as a social advancement within capitalism but with various post-capitalistic aspects in need of protection, enforcement, stimulation and connection with progressive social movements. Using a four-scenario approach, we attempt to simplify possible outcomes and to explore relevant trajectories of the current techno-economic paradigm within and beyond capitalism. The first part of the book begins with an introduction (Chapters 1 and 2) of the techno-economic paradigm shifts theory, which sees capitalism as a creative destruction process. Such a dynamic, innovation-based understanding of economic and societal development arguably allows for an integral bird's-eye view of future scenarios (Chapter 3) within and beyond the dominant system. Sharing the conviction that the globalized economy is at a critical turning point, we describe the four future scenarios: netarchical capitalism, distributed capitalism, resilient communities and global Commons. Netarchical and distributed capitalism (Chapters 4 and 5) are parts of the wider value mode of cognitive capitalism and form, what we call 'the mixed model of neo-feudal cognitive capitalism' (Chapter 6). On the other hand, the resilient communities (Chapter 7) and the global Commons (Chapter 8) reside in the

DOI: 10.1057/9781137406897.0003

hypothetical model of mature peer production under civic dominance. We postulate that the mature peer production communities pose a sustainable alternative to capital accumulation, that of the circulation of the Commons. Hence, we make some tentative transition proposals toward a Commons-based economy and society for the state, the market and the civic domain (Chapter 9). Finally, we conclude with remarks and suggestions for future actions.

DOI: 10.1057/9781137406897.0003

Acknowledgments

We would like to express our very great appreciation to Christos Giotitsas, Denis Postle, Katarzyna Gajewska, Helene Finidori and Nikos Anastasopoulos for their constructive suggestions during the planning and development of this research work. In addition to this, we are particularly indebted to Vasilis Niaros for his support in the editing of the book as well as in the designing of the figures. Further, we owe gratitude to Wolfgang Drechsler, Nikos Salingaros, Rainer Kattel and Carlota Perez who have been mentoring our work for years now. Moreover, we would like to extend our thanks to Ann Marie and Stacco from Guerrilla Translation! for carefully copy-editing the text; as well as to Christina Brian, Head of Politics & International Studies at Palgrave Macmillan, and Ambra Finotello, editorial assistant, for their constant support, understanding and eagerness. Also, the work of the FLOK Society, a collaborative research effort in Ecuador, has been crucial to develop transition and policy proposals toward a Commons-based knowledge society. Michel Bauwens was the research director of the FLOK society project and Vasilis Kostakis served as an external collaborator. The latter also acknowledges financial support by the 'Challenges to State Modernization in 21st Century Europe' Estonian Institutional Grant [IUT 19-13] and the 'Web 2.0 and Governance: Institutional and Normative Changes and Challenges' Estonian Research Foundation grant [ETF 8571]. We dedicate this work to all those who are building the world they want, within the confines of the world they want to transcend.

DOI: 10.1057/9781137406897.0004

Part I
Theoretical Framework

DOI: 10.1057/9781137406897.0005

1

Capitalism as a Creative Destruction System

Abstracts: *Many would argue that no other economic system than capitalism has produced so much wealth. On the other hand, some might claim that no other system has produced so much destruction. Others consider capitalism as a creative destruction system. This chapter discusses the theory of techno-economic paradigm shifts with the aim to recognize the dynamic nature of the capitalist system, and highlight the transition potential of new modes of social production and organization. Kostakis and Bauwens argue that the world is at a turning point where the excesses, the fallacies and the unsustainability of the current practices have to be recognized and appropriate regulatory changes have to be made, so that desperation and anger are turned into creation.*

Kostakis, Vasilis and Michel Bauwens. *Network Society and Future Scenarios for a Collaborative Economy*. Basingstoke: Palgrave Macmillan, 2014. DOI: 10.1057/9781137406897.0006.

The capitalist mode of production has arguably created a political economy prone to crises. Following Harvey's (2012, p. 5) vivid narration, a typical day in the life of a capitalist begins with a certain amount of money and ends with a lot more. The next day, however, the capitalist has to think about how he is going to manage that surplus capital: will he reinvest the profits or will he spend them? As long as we are not speaking about monopolies (Baran and Sweezy, 1966), the fierce competition compels him to reinvest. If he does not, a competitor certainly will. Of course, a successful capitalist profits enough to maintain profitable expansion while also living a super-luxurious life. The constant search for new terrains of growth is a premise for the sustainability of the system. Capital accumulation must expand at a compound rate; according to Harvey (2012, p. 5), 'the result of perpetual reinvestment is the expansion of surplus production'. The capitalist faces a variety of problems during the aforementioned procedure. If wages were too high due to labor scarcity, for instance, fresh labor forces must be found or precarious living conditions must be artificially created, thus inducing a drop in wages, in order to keep the system in a growth trajectory. Furthermore, that new terrain of growth is enriched with the introduction of new means of production and technological and/or organizational innovations. New needs and wants are defined, distances between nation-states diminished, and the capitalist finds himself capable not only of discovering new natural resources but also of attracting new customers (Harvey, 2012, 2010; Perez, 2002). When purchasing power cannot serve an increasingly expanding economy, new credit-based financial instruments are invented. If the profit rate is low, sometimes companies merge, creating powerful conglomerates and, therefore, monopolies. If capital accumulation does not continue, then the system falls into a crisis: Capitalists are unable to find profitable paths of reinvestment; capital accumulation stagnates and its value decreases; massive unemployment, impoverishment and social turmoil are some of the potential consequences of a capitalist crisis.

But many would argue that no other economic system has produced so much wealth. On the other hand, some might claim that no other system has produced so much destruction. Others consider capitalism a creative destruction system. This book uses the theory of techno-economic paradigm shifts (TEPS) – gradually developed by Schumpeter (1982/1939, 1975/1942), Kondratieff (1979), Freeman (1974, 1996), and in particular Perez (1983, 1985, 1988, 2002, 2009a, 2009b) – as its point of departure to develop its narrative. This choice arguably helps to recognize the dynamic

DOI: 10.1057/9781137406897.0006

and changing nature of the capitalist system, in order to avoid any particular period of extrapolation as 'the end of history' in the fashion of Fukuyama (1992). Therefore, the aim is not to make capitalism crisis-free but to manage crises and soften blows. In other words, to form a successful 'creative destruction management' (Kalvet and Kattel, 2006), maximizing its creative power while minimizing its destructive force (Mulgan, 2013). One should be aware of many other theoretical alternatives, those of Marx for example, in understanding and acting within certain social, technological and economic processes. Interestingly, Marxist and neo-Schumpeterian theoretical approaches consider capitalism prone to crises, which are basic features of its normal functioning. However, the neo-Marxist critique (see Wolff, 2010; Harvey, 2007, 2010) puts emphasis on the inherent unsustainability of capitalism, aiming at a different system – 'modern society can do better than capitalism', Wolff (2010) postulates – whereas neo-Schumpeterians, such as Perez (2002) or Freeman (1974; 1996), see crises as a chance to move the capitalist economy forward. This book is an integrative attempt at highlighting the potential of new modes of social production and organization immanent in capitalism but which, in the long term, might transcend the dominant system.

If we follow Schmoller (1898/1893), the main figure of the German Historical School, history is the laboratory of the economist. Despite the unquestionable uniqueness of each historical period in socio-economic development, the theory of TEPS accepts recurrence as a frame of reference and, having each period's uniqueness as the object of study, tries to interpret the potential and the direction of change (Perez, 2002). Moreover, it embraces the Schumpeterian (1982/1939) understanding of economy as 'an interdependent sequence of dynamic forces of change and static equilibrating forces' (Drechsler et al., 2006, p. 15). The essential fact about capitalism is the process of creative destruction incessantly revolutionizing the economic structure from within, destroying the old one while creating a new one (Schumpeter, 1975/1942). Each techno-economic paradigm (TEP) is based on a constellation of innovations, both technical and organizational, which are the driving force behind economic development (Perez, 1983). Each TEP plays the central role in a recurring pattern of cyclical movement: from gilded ages to golden ages; from an initial installation period, through a collapse and recession that signify the turning point, to a full deployment period (Perez, 2002, 2009a). Therefore, in the Perezian framework (2002, 2009a), progress in capitalism takes place by going through various successive

DOI: 10.1057/9781137406897.0006

great surges of development which are driven by successive technological revolutions. Each of these overlapping great surges of development,
lasting approximately 40–60 years, is the process by which a technological revolution and its paradigm propagate across the economy, 'leading
to structural changes in production, distribution, communication and
consumption as well as to profound and qualitative changes in society'
(Perez, 2002, p. 15).

According to the TEPS theory, the world has experienced five technological revolutions during the past three centuries: the first industrial
revolution based on machines, factories and canals (initiated in 1771;
birthplace: Britain); the age of steam, coal, iron and railways (1829;
Britain); the age of steel and heavy engineering (1875; Britain, USA, and
Germany); the age of automobile, oil, petrochemicals and mass production (1908; USA); and the age of information technology and communication (1971; USA). Each of these processes evolved 'from small beginnings
in restricted sectors and geographic regions', and ended up 'encompassing
the bulk of activities in the core country or countries and diffusing out
towards further and further peripheries, depending on the capacity of the
transport and communications infrastructures' (Perez, 2002, p. 15).

A great surge of development consists of four phases, which, although
not strictly separated, can be identified as sharing common characteristics throughout history (Figure 1.1).

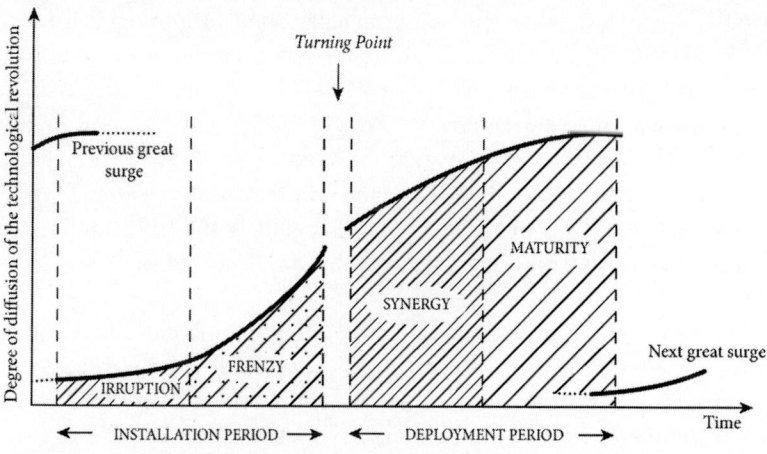

FIGURE 1.1   *Recurring phases of each great surge in the core countries*

Source: Based on Perez, C. (2002) *Technological Revolutions and Financial Capital: The
Dynamics of Bubbles and Golden Ages* (Cheltenham: Edward Elgar Pub), p. 48.

DOI: 10.1057/9781137406897.0006

First, we have irruption (technological explosion), or the initial development of new technologies in a world where the bulk of the economy is made of old, maturing and declining industries. Frenzy follows, which is the rapid development of technology requiring a great deal of finance (this is when financial bubbles are created). These two first phases constitute the installation period of the new TEP, when finance and greed prevail and the paper economy decouples from the real one. Next, turbulent times arrive – that is, collapse, recession and instability. This is what Perez calls the turning point: neither a phase nor an event, but rather a process of contextual shift, where institutional changes for the deployment period of the newly installed paradigm take place. Institutional innovations occur, which enable economies to take advantage of new technology across all sectors, and in turn to spread the benefits of this new wealth-creating potential widely across society. These synergies appear in the early stages of deployment (synergy phase) until they approach a ceiling (maturity phase) in productivity, new products and markets. Once that ceiling is hit, social unrest and confrontations will occur while conditions for the installation of the new paradigm, based on the next technological revolution, are set.

Perez (2009b) highlights the special nature of major technological bubbles (MTB), which are endogenous to the process by which society and the economy assimilate each great surge. The MTB tend to take place along the diffusion path of each technological revolution: from the installation period, when the new constellation of technologies is tested and investment is defined by the short-term goals of financial capital (so a rift between real values and paper values occurs), to the deployment period, when financial capital is brought back to reality, production capital takes the lead and the state is called to make effective 'creative destruction management' (Kalvet and Kattel, 2006). Perez (2009b) argues that the MTB of the current TEP, that is the information and communications technology (ICT) revolution, occurred in two episodes (Figure 1.2).

First was the Internet mania, based on technological innovation, which ended in the NASDAQ collapse in 2000. This was followed by the easy liquidity bubble, based on financial innovations accelerated by the new technologies, ending in the financial crisis in 2007–08. The essential implication of Perez' (2009b, p. 803) argumentation is that 'what we are facing is not just a financial crisis but rather the end of a period and the need for a structural shift in social and economic context to allow for

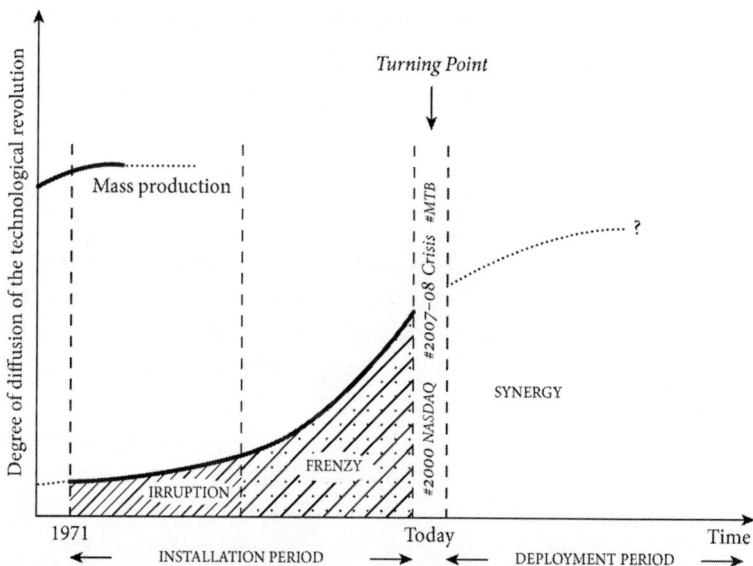

FIGURE 1.2   *The current ICT-driven techno-economic paradigm: The major technological bubbles at the turning point and a deployment period to come*

Source: Based on Perez, C. (2002) *Technological Revolutions and Financial Capital: The Dynamics of Bubbles and Golden Ages* (Cheltenham: Edward Elgar Pub), p. 48.

continued growth under this paradigm'. Moreover, Perez' (2009b) essay on the double bubble, aligned with the TEPS theory, is used as a point of departure that treats the current situation as not just another passing recession, and sets the ground for tentative proposals concerning the second half of the ICT revolution's wealth-generating potential.

Since the introduction of the microprocessor (California, November, 1971), and after a nearly 30-year-long paroxystic culmination of market experimentation and moments of Galbraithian (1993) irrationality, we find ourselves in the aftermath of two major bubbles and, arguably, in the midst of a major capitalist crisis (Fuchs et al., 2010, p. 193). In other words, we are witnessing, as we will later see, the swing of the pendulum from extreme individualism to collective, synergistic well-being. The whole system is trying to recompose (Perez, 2002), while political unrest (e.g., the EU coherency crisis triggered by the debt crisis) and protests (from the Indignados movement in Spain and the protest movement in Greece to the Occupy Wall Street movement in the USA) are erupting

DOI: 10.1057/9781137406897.0006

globally. However, this book's goal is neither to describe the strands and ramifications of the current crisis, as this has been done elsewhere (see Harvey, 2007, 2010; Chomsky, 2011; Funnell, Jupe and Andrew, 2009; Stiglitz, 2010), nor to indicate historical parallels in previous turning points within capitalism, as Perez has done that in detail in her 2002 book. It can be claimed, though, that the two bubbles at the turn of this century recall the 1929 depression in that they share one fundamental characteristic: the structural tensions within capitalism make the system, at least in its current form, unsustainable. The world is arguably at a crossroads where the excesses, the fallacies and the unsustainability of the current practices need to be recognized; appropriate regulatory changes have to be made where the usual recipes for confronting tensions fail; and conditions where production capital is put in control, greater social cohesion is achieved, and desperation and anger turn into creation must be facilitated (Perez, 2002, 2009a, 2009b). In other words, this turning point is a time of indeterminate realization of the full potential of the current ICT-driven paradigm, creating the new fabric of the economy and overcoming the tensions that caused this premature saturation (Perez, 2002).

DOI: 10.1057/9781137406897.0006

2
Beyond the End of History: Three Competing Value Models

Abstract: *At the current turning point of the ICT-based techno-economic paradigm and within the present political economy, this chapter argues, there are three different value models competing for dominance, which influence the way that the institutional recompositions will take place. One form is still dominant, but rapidly declining in importance; a second form is reaching dominance; and a third is emerging. This chapter discusses the decline of the first competing value model, that of the classic capitalist economy based on labor value and proprietary forms of knowledge.*

Kostakis, Vasilis and Michel Bauwens. *Network Society and Future Scenarios for a Collaborative Economy*. Basingstoke: Palgrave Macmillan, 2014. DOI: 10.1057/9781137406897.0007.

Have we already lived through the end of history with the fall of the Berlin wall in 1989–90? Is the capitalist mode of production in the final stage of human progress? Or are we currently living in the end times with capitalism approaching its terminal crisis? According to Žižek (2010, p. x), the dominant system is unable to face its internal imbalances and its failures: the ongoing ecological crisis as well as the emergence of new forms of apartheid, walls and slums. Capitalism transforms not because of its failures but because of its successes, neo-Schumpeterians might reply, and now it is high time we created virtuous circles of production that would allow the system to reinvent itself once again. The environmental crisis can be seen as an opportunity for investment and sustainable growth (Gore, 2013). In the meantime, a new type of capitalism, named 'cognitive capitalism', arises in which 'the object of accumulation consists mainly of knowledge' that is now the basic source of value (Boutang, 2012, p. 57). The industrial mode of production is becoming obsolete, and the 'network' is the main pattern of organizing production and socio-political relations (see Castells, 2000, 2003, 2009). Peer-to-peer (P2P) technologies and renewable energy merge, creating an energy Internet and, thus, inaugurating a third industrial revolution (Rifkin, 2011). On top of that, one may add another disruptive technological cluster, the 'Internet of Things', which could help 'humanity reintegrate itself into the complex choreography of the biosphere, and by doing so, dramatically increases productivity without compromising the ecological relationships that govern the planet' (Rifkin, 2014, p. 13). Others (see Anderson, 2012) point to emerging desktop manufacturing technologies, such as the three dimensional (3D) printing, and consider them the pervasive technological cluster which will trigger a new industrial revolution. Success in taking advantage of these transformations, and, at least in theory, the benefits of new wealth creating potential will spread more widely across society.

This book argues that, at the current turning point of the ICT-based TEP and within the present political economy, there are three different value models competing for dominance, which influence the way institutional recompositions will take place. One form is still dominant, but rapidly declining in importance; a second form is reaching dominance, but carries within itself the seeds of its own destruction; and a third is emerging, but needs vital new policies in order to become dominant (Figure 2.1).

DOI: 10.1057/9781137406897.0007

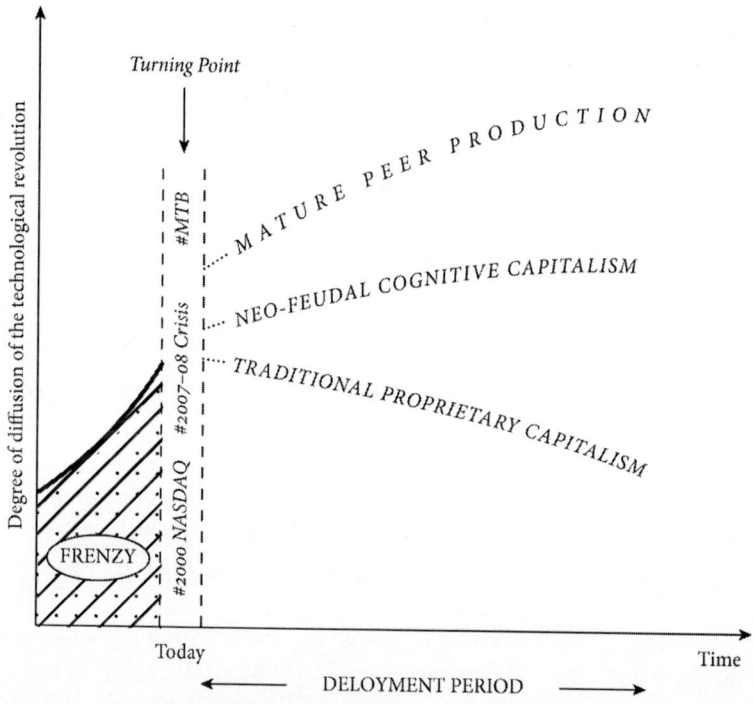

FIGURE 2.1 *Three competing value models*

The first is the classic capitalist economy based on labor value and proprietary forms of knowledge, which dominated the industrial phase of capitalism. The value model of the traditional proprietary capitalism is based on the premise that workers create value in their private capacity as providers of labor (Figure 2.2). This value is captured and realized in the market by capital, which dominates the extraction of surplus value. In the old neoliberal vision, the state becomes a market state which protects the privileged interests of property owners; and civil society is a 'rest category' – a sphere of minor importance as is evidenced in the use of our language (nonprofits, nongovernmental). The de-skilling of workers – what was once artisanal production knowledge but which is now codified in the production process itself – characterizes this form. Labor becomes an appendage to the ecosystem of machines. In this division between labor and capital, managerial and engineering layers handle collective production on behalf of the owners of capital. At first,

DOI: 10.1057/9781137406897.0007

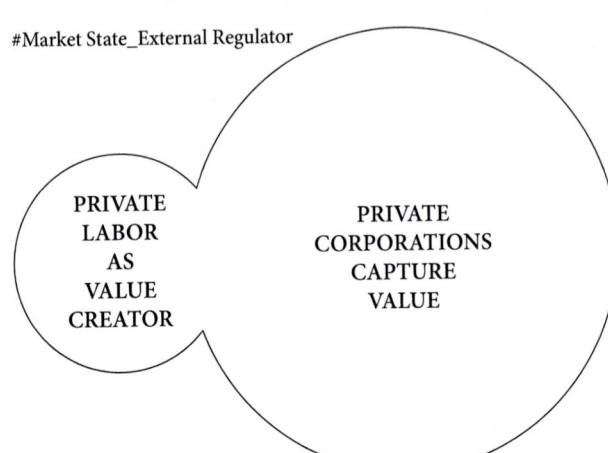

FIGURE 2.2   *The value model of the traditional proprietary capitalism which dominated the first phase of the current techno-economic paradigm*

this is largely industrial capital, though financial capital rises rapidly to prominence. Codified knowledge is proprietary and value is increasingly captured as intellectual property (IP) rent. However, industrial profit, based on the direct extraction of surplus value, is the dominant form of value capture, and there is partial redistribution in the form of wages.

Often, once a social (labor) movement takes form and becomes powerful and influential, the state redistributes taxable wealth to the workers as consumers and citizens in the form of social provisions (pensions, unemployment benefits, health care reimbursements etc.). This happened extensively during 1945–80, manifested by the rise of the welfare state and Keynesian policies, especially in the Western world. Since 1980, under contemporary conditions of labor weakness in the de-industrializing developed countries, the state has been redistributing wealth to the financial sector and creating conditions of debt dependence for the majority of the population. In this neoliberal format, which became dominant after 1980 before the emergence of civic peer networks on the eve of the 21st century (Benkler, 2006; Bauwens, 2005), the part of labor became stagnant and most of the value was streamed toward financial capital. The credit system developed into an increasingly important means to maintain the fictitious buying power of consumers

DOI: 10.1057/9781137406897.0007

and, therefore, the primary means of surplus realization through debt dependency and servicing.

We argue that this value model of traditional proprietary capitalism, dominant in the installation period of the current TEP, is approaching its terminal point. Its inherent unsustainability is manifested in a twofold problem. On the one hand, industrial capitalism considers nature to be a perpetually abundant resource; that is, it is based on a false notion of material abundance in a finite world. On the other hand, the traditional, industrial version of cognitive capitalism enforces the idea that intellectual, scientific and technical exchange should be subject to strong proprietary constraints. In that way, an artificial scarcity of knowledge is created, subjecting innovation to legal restrictions and allowing for profit maximization and, hence, capital accumulation. Thus appears the paradoxical but also dramatic contradiction of the present, dominant system: while it is rapidly overburdening the carrying capacity of the planet, it simultaneously inhibits the solutions humanity might find for it. For example, the dramatic increase in patents has not been paralleled by an increase in technological innovation: 'there is no empirical evidence that they [patents] serve to increase innovation and productivity, unless productivity [or innovation] is identified with the number of patents awarded' (Boldrin and Levine, 2013, p. 3). 'In the long run', Boldrin and Levine (2013, p. 7) argue, 'patents reduce the incentives for current innovation because current innovators are subject to constant legal action and licensing demands from earlier patent holders.' The process of innovation relies upon building on former innovations. Therefore, the broader the pool of accessible ideas, the more chances there are for innovation (Brynjolfsson and McAfee, 2011). To recap, this combination of quasi-abundance and quasi-scarcity destroys the biosphere and hampers the expansion of social innovation and a 'free culture' (as described in Lessig, 2004), and this situation, arguably, must be reversed.

The recent crises have brought scholars from various traditions and schools to agree that the global economy is currently at a turning point within the ICT-driven TEP. In this book, we deal with the remaining two competing value models. These are more synchronized with the main characteristics of the current TEP, and they seem to introduce less-fragile alternative approaches for development in the deployment period. The second form is the neo-feudal cognitive capitalism, in which proprietary forms of knowledge are in the process of being displaced by emerging

DOI: 10.1057/9781137406897.0007

forms of peer production (Benkler, 2006; Bauwens, 2005), but under the dominance of financial capital. We will describe how this process is well under way. The third is the hypothetical form of mature peer production under civic dominance, whose stems are already emerging through the interstices of the dominant system.

DOI: 10.1057/9781137406897.0007

3
The P2P Infrastructures: Two Axes and Four Quadrants

Abstract: *The P2P infrastructures, such as the Internet, are those infrastructures for communication, cooperation and common value creation that allow for permission-less interlinking of human cooperators and their technological aids. It has been assumed that such infrastructures are becoming the general conditions of work, life and society. In this context, this chapter introduces a four-scenario approach which attempts to simplify possible outcomes by using two axes or polarities (global versus local orientation; centralized versus distributed control of the infrastructure). Each quadrant stands for a certain scenario where each technological regime (namely, netarchical capitalism, distributed capitalism, resilient communities, and global Commons) is dominant.*

Kostakis, Vasilis and Michel Bauwens. *Network Society and Future Scenarios for a Collaborative Economy*. Basingstoke: Palgrave Macmillan, 2014. DOI: 10.1057/9781137406897.0008.

The P2P infrastructures, such as the Internet, are those infrastructures for communication, cooperation and common value creation that allow for permission-less interlinking of human cooperators and their technological aids. We argue that such infrastructures are becoming the general conditions of work, life and society (see Bauwens, 2005). Of course, one should be aware of the danger of 'Internet-centrism' (Morozov, 2012) and the perception that the Internet is the solution to all of humanity's problems. However, change is unlikely to occur without sufficient ICT penetration since, as has become evident, various aspects of complex human nature can be amplified and telescoped by the Internet (MacKinnon, 2012). P2P relational dynamics, which sometimes seem to epitomize the old slogan 'Jeder nach seinen Fähigkeiten, jedem nach seinen Bedürfnissen!' [from each according to his ability, to each according to his need], are based on the distribution of the productive forces. First, the means of information, immaterial production, that is the networked computers, and now the means of physical manufacturing, that is, machines that produce physical objects, are being distributed and interconnected. Just as networked computers democratized the means of production of information and communication, the emergent elements of networked micro-factories or what some (see Kostakis, Fountouklis and Drechsler, 2013; Anderson, 2012; Rifkin, 2014) call desktop manufacturing, such as 3D printing and computer-numerical-control (CNC) machines, are democratizing the means of making.

Of course, this process is not without its problems. In a time of extreme polarization and with no equilibrium reached in regard to global governance of the Internet (Mueller, 2010), we have witnessed conflicts over the control and ownership of distributed infrastructures. For example, the Internet, the world's largest ungoverned space (Schmidt and Cohen, 2013), has become a highly contested political space (MacKinnon, 2012). On the one side, peer production signals for some fundamental changes to take place juxtaposing them against an old order that should be cast off (Bauwens, 2005; Benkler, 2006). On the other, the proposed legislations of ACTA/SOPA/PIPA that enforce strict copyright; the attempts at surveillance, public opinion manipulation, censorship and the marginalization of opposite voices by both authoritarian and liberal countries (MacKinnon, 2012); and 'the growing tendency to link the Internet's security problems to the very properties that made it innovative and revolutionary in the first place' (Mueller, 2010, p. 160) are only some of the reasons that have made some scholars (see Zittrain, 2008; MacKinnon, 2012) worry that digital systems may be pushed back to the model of locked-down devices or centrally controlled information appliances. Hence, there appears to be a battle emerging among agents (several governments and corporations), which are trying to turn the Internet into a tightly controlled information medium, and user communities who are trying to keep the medium independent.

This book attempts to simplify possible outcomes by using two axes, or polarities, which give rise to four possible scenarios. Each quadrant stands for a certain scenario where each technological regime is dominant. This does not exclude the presence of the rest; however, the dominant regime defines the kind of political economy which may prevail. Value regimes are more or less associated with technology regimes, since the forces at play want to protect their interests through the control of technological and media platforms, which encourage certain behaviors and logics, but discourage others. The powers over technological protocols and value-driven design decisions are used to create technological platforms that match proprietary interests. Even as P2P technologies and networks are becoming ubiquitous, ostensibly similar P2P technologies have very different characteristics which lead to different models of value creation and distribution, and thus to different social and technological behaviors. In networks, human behavior can be subtly – or not so subtly – influenced by design decisions and invisible protocols created in the interest of the owners or managers of the platforms.

Figure 3.1 is organized around two axes, which determine at least four distinct possibilities. The first top-down axis distinguishes centralized technological control (and an orientation toward globality) from distributed technological control (and an orientation toward localization); the horizontal axis distinguishes a for-profit orientation (where any social good is subsumed to the goal of shareholder profit), from for-benefit orientations (where eventual profits are subsumed to the social goal).

The four-scenario approach has been widely used as an exploratory tool that allows for fruitful discussions on policymaking (van der Heijden, 2005; Leigh, 2003) and sustainable strategic planning and development (Godet, 2000; Kelly, Sirr and Ratcliffe, 2004). Each scenario has a descriptive role and outlines tentative political economies with the aim of sparking the imagination and serving as a route map for the future

DOI: 10.1057/9781137406897.0008

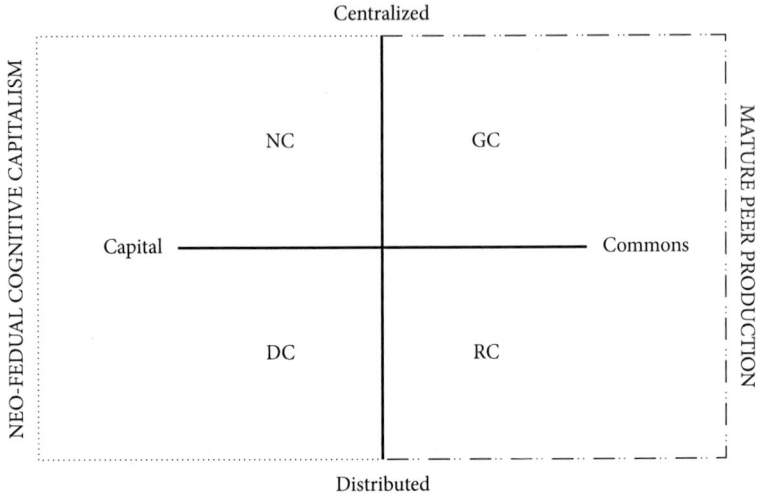

FIGURE 3.1   *Two axes and four future scenarios*

(Miles, 2004). Using scenarios is like rehearsing the future, according to Schwartz (1996). By rehearsing these future scenarios, organizations, states and the civil society can adapt to what is happening and anticipate and influence what could transpire. In accordance with van der Heijden et al. (2002) and Schwartz (1996), our scenario framework consists of two dimensions which have high levels of uncertainty and are crucial to future developments. The first axis presents the polarity of centralized versus distributed control of the productive infrastructure, whereas the second axis relates an orientation toward the accumulation of capital versus an orientation toward the accumulation or circulation of the Commons.

Within this context the following four future scenarios for economy and society are introduced: netarchical capitalism (NC), distributed capitalism (DC), resilient communities (RC) and global Commons (GC). Netarchical and distributed capitalism differ in the control of the productive infrastructure but both are oriented toward capital accumulation and, thus, are parts of the wider value mode of cognitive capitalism. They actually form the mixed model of neo-feudal cognitive capitalism. On the other, resilient communities and the global Commons reside in the, one might say auspicious, hypothetical model of mature peer production under civic dominance (right quadrants). The next parts shed

DOI: 10.1057/9781137406897.0008

light on each scenario in separate chapters, also discussing the coexistence of each pair of models sharing a common orientation. Moreover, Part III attempts to introduce a few preliminary general principles for policymaking, and put forward some general policy recommendations with the goal of moving from the left side of the quadrants to the right. Or, to put it in the terms of the TEPS theory, to realize the full potential of an ICT-driven TEP while maximizing the benefits from technological progress for the largest part of society.

DOI: 10.1057/9781137406897.0008

Part II
Cognitive Capitalism

Cognitive capitalism refers to the process by which information (data, knowledge, design or culture) is privatized and then commodified as a means of generating profit for capital. In this new phase of capitalism, traditional processes of material production and distribution are overtaken by the control of information as the driving force of capital accumulation (see Boutang, 2012; Bell, 1973; Drucker, 1969; for a critical analysis, see Webster, 2006). Of course, we should be aware of Federici and Caffentzis' (2007, p. 70) remark that notions such as 'cognitive labor' and 'cognitive capitalism' represent 'a part, though a leading one, of capitalist development and that different forms of knowledge and cognitive work exist that cannot be flattened under one label'. In general, one could argue that capitalism, in the past, was primarily concerned with the commodification of material. Essential to this process was the gradual enclosure and privatization of the material Commons, including pasture lands, forests and waterways that had been used in common since time immemorial (for an analysis of the 1700–1820 enclosure in England, see Neeson, 1993). In our time, capitalism entails the enclosure and commodification of the immaterial: knowledge, culture, DNA, airwaves, even ideas (for an account of the 'second enclosure movement', see Boyle, 2003b). Ultimately, the driving force of capitalism in our age is the eradication

DOI: 10.1057/9781137406897.0009

of all Commons and the commodification of all things. The colonization and appropriation of the public domain by capital is arguably at the heart of the new enclosures. This process is sustained and extended through the complex and ever-evolving web of patents, copyright laws, trade agreements, think tanks, and government and academic institutions that provide the legal, policy and ideological frameworks that justify all this (for a critical perspective on strict intellectual property see Lessig, 2004; Boldrin and Levine, 2013; Patry, 2009; Bessen and Meuer, 2009). Above all, the logic of this process is embedded in the values, organization and operation of the traditional capitalist firm.

In the new vision of cognitive capitalism, which represents this book's second competing value model, networked social cooperation consists of mostly unpaid activities that can be captured and financialized by proprietary 'network' platforms. Social media platforms almost exclusively capture the value of their members' social exchange, and distributed labor, such as crowdsourcing, tends to reduce the average income of the producers (for an overview of crowdsourcing's labor markets, digital labor and the dark side of the Internet in general, see the collective book edited by Scholz, 2012). The 'netarchical' (meaning, the hierarchies within the network which own and control participatory platforms) version of networked production, here, creates a permanent precariat and reinforces the neoliberal trends. Projects such as the P2P currency Bitcoin and the Kickstarter crowdfunding platform are representative examples of more distributed developments which embrace the idea that 'everyone can become an independent capitalist'. Under this model, P2P infrastructures are designed to allow the autonomy and participation of many players, but the main focus is still profit maximization. Next we deal with the two forms of the neo-feudal model of cognitive capitalism (left quadrants), which are based on various technological regimes dependent on the structure of every project's back-end. User-oriented technological systems generally have two sides. The front-end is the side that users interact with, and is the only side visible to them. In other words, it is the interface with the other users and with the system itself. The back-end, however, is the technological underpinning that makes it all possible. This is engineered by the platform owners and is invisible to the user. Hence, a front-end which enables a P2P social logic among users can often be highly centralized, controlled, and proprietary on the back-end; forming an invisible techno-social system that profoundly influences the behavior of those using the front-end, by setting limits on

DOI: 10.1057/9781137406897.0009

what is possible in terms of human freedom. As we will see in Chapters 4 and 5, a truly free P2P logic at the front-end is highly improbable if the back-end is under exclusive control and ownership. This part concludes with Chapter 6, where the potentialities of this value model are discussed.

DOI: 10.1057/9781137406897.0009

4
Netarchical Capitalism

Abstract: *This chapter describes the first technological regime/future scenario which develops within the context of a new-feudal form of cognitive capitalism. 'Netarchical capitalism' matches centralized control of a distributed infrastructure with an orientation toward the accumulation of capital. For Kostakis and Bauwens, the netarchical capital is that fraction of capital which enables cooperation, but through proprietary platforms that are under central control. While individuals share through these platforms, they have no control over the design and the protocol of these networks/platforms, which are proprietary. Typically under conditions of netarchical capitalism, while sharers directly create or share use value, the monetized exchange value is realized by the owners of capital. This arguably creates a longer-term 'value crisis', since the value creators are not rewarded.*

Kostakis, Vasilis and Michel Bauwens. *Network Society and Future Scenarios for a Collaborative Economy.* Basingstoke: Palgrave Macmillan, 2014. DOI: 10.1057/9781137406897.0010.

The period since the 1990s saw the birth of a mixed regime. Civic inter-networks (systems of interconnected networks) became increasingly available to a wider population, and other forms of networked value creation became possible. Use value has been created independently of the private industrial and financial system, through different forms of peer production and networked value creation. This creative process has taken place in the form of civic contributions, where immaterial use value is deposited in common pools of knowledge, code and design. In 'pure' peer production, this immaterial value is contributed and deposited into common pools by voluntary or paid contributors. The for-benefit associations, such as the Free/Libre/Open Source Software (FLOSS) foundations, enable continued cooperation; and entrepreneurial coalitions of mostly for-profit capitalist enterprise capture the added value in the marketplace. For example, the cases of the International Business Machines corporation (IBM) and Linux is well-known and widely discussed (see Tapscott and Williams, 2006; Coleman and Hill, 2004; IBM, 2010). This coalition shows how a firm entered the FLOSS ecology and invested monetary and human capital (improving the reliability of Linux by testing code, error handling etc.) in the development of FLOSS. IBM, according to its corporate report (2010), holds significant roles in a large number of FLOSS projects such as in the development of the Linux Kernel, Apache, Eclipse or Ubuntu, working closely with Red Hat, a leading distributor of the Linux enterprise. On the one hand, IBM's involvement enhanced the quality of the outputs and the sustainability of the projects, creating chances for wage labor for some of the most active and skillful Linux developers in the market economy. On the other, the rewards from such an involvement have been considerable for IBM. According to Tapscott and Williams (at least at the time of their writing in 2006) the firm would spend about $100 million per year on general Linux development. So if the Linux community produces use value of $1 billion (if it were to be produced by paid labor), and even half of that is useful to IBM, then the firm gains $500 million of software development for an investment of $100 million (Tapscott and Williams, 2006). 'Linux gives us a viable platform uniquely tailored to our needs for twenty percent of the cost of a proprietary OS' says Cawley, IBM's business development executive at that time, in Tapscott and Williams (2006, p. 81). To put the matter bluntly, IBM would pay $2 to ten employees but would get a value of more than $20 by many more than ten contributors, from whom a considerable number would participate on a voluntary basis. In this model,

DOI: 10.1057/9781137406897.0010

there is a continued creation of use value in the public sphere and, thus, an accumulation or a circulation of the Commons based on open input, participatory processes of production and Commons-oriented output. However, the accumulation of capital still continues through the form of labor and capital in the entrepreneurial coalitions. It becomes obvious that an increasing amount of voluntary labor is extracted in this process.

In the so-called sharing economies of networked value characterized by networking processes which take place over proprietary platforms, the use value is created by the social media users, but their attention is what creates a marketplace where that use value becomes extracted exchange value. In the realm of exchange value, this new form of netarchical capitalism may be interpreted as hyper-exploitation, since the use value creators go totally unrewarded in terms of exchange value, which is solely realized by the proprietary platforms. For instance, Facebook and Google, perhaps the two bigger netarchical capitalists, abandon direct production and instead create and maintain platforms which allow people to produce. They rely much more marginally on IP protection, but rather allow P2P communication while controlling its potential monetization through their ownership of the platforms for such communication. Typically, the front-end is P2P, in that it allows P2P sociality, but the back-end is controlled. The design is in the hands of the owners, as are the private data of the users, and it is the attention of the user-base that is marketed through advertising. The financialization of cooperation is still the name of the game. The back-end of these platforms, which serve as attention pools, is generally a centralized system where personal data is privatized. The monetization of the surplus value produced is exclusionary, keeping the users/producers out of that process. Almost everything is controlled by the owners of the platforms and there is an unequal distribution of power among owners and users. The same applies in other proprietary platforms, such as Airbnb, a platform that helps people to rent out lodging, including private rooms, entire apartments, boats, tree houses, private islands and other properties. In other words, it commodifies things, that is, idle resources, that were not previously commodified. If one looks carefully at the back-end of Airbnb's productive structure, he/she would realize that there is neither collaborative production nor governance, and the control rests with the owners of the platform. In essence, platform owners, who are crucially dependent on the trust of user communities, exploit the aggregated attention and input

DOI: 10.1057/9781137406897.0010

of the networks in different ways, even as they enable it. In addition, such platforms are dangerous as trustees of any common value that might be created, due to their speculative nature and the opaque architecture (closed source) of their platforms (Kostakis, 2012). The parasitic nature of this mode becomes evident by the fact that an empty networking platform is arguably a valueless platform. In addition to this, search engines and social networks limit the diversity of information sources so as to please their advertising customers, potentially minimizing the development of critically thinking citizens (Pariser, 2011). To recap, we call 'aggregated distribution' the productive models which are followed by corporations such as Google, Facebook, Airbnb or even IBM. Of course, it is important to emphasize that each netarchical project has its own special characteristics and peculiarities and it is difficult, if not impossible, to provide an all-inclusive description. However, what these projects have in common is that while their front-ends (whether the platform's infrastructure, see Facebook or Airbnb, or a P2P practice that the company may follow, see IBM) might be distributed, they are based on certain technological regimes of centralized back-ends while having a for-profit orientation with exclusionary financialization (Figure 4.1).

Further, in the form of crowdsourced marketplaces, capital abandons the labor form and externalizes risk onto the freelancers. Crowdsourcing

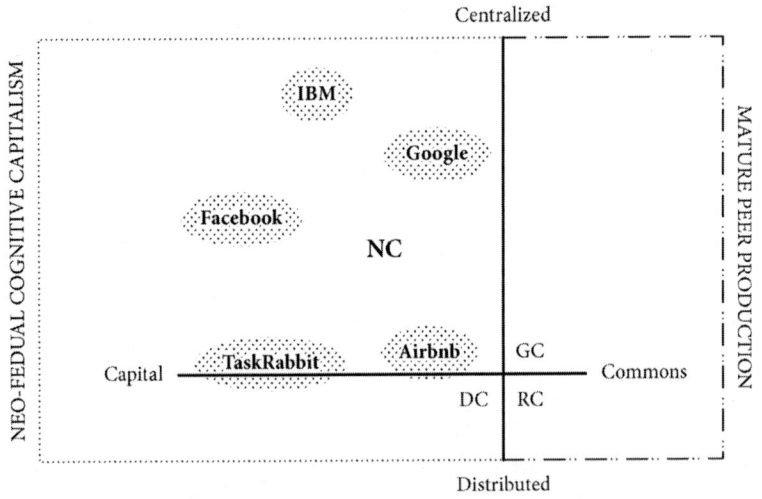

FIGURE 4.1   *The netarchical capitalism quadrant*

DOI: 10.1057/9781137406897.0010

economies are not very different to the sharing ones in that users still 'share' information, in a way. Compared with the sharing/aggregation economies, the profit motive for users is a bit stronger here, mainly in the form of a prize (Kostakis, 2012). Howe (2008) offers case histories such as iStock, a community-driven source for stock photography, and InnoCentive, where firms offer cash prizes for solving some of their thorniest development problems. Other crowdsourcing platforms include 99designs and DesignCrowd, which both deal with design (from logo design to T-shirt design). We consider crowdsourcing projects as 'disaggregated distribution', because the workers are isolated freelancers competing without collective shared IP. For instance, think of a crowd-sourced logo production: the crowdsourcing company will choose the best logo out of, say, 50 logos, and the remaining 49 will often be trashed. No production of common, shared value takes place. Another typical example could be the 'skills' marketplace TaskRabbit, where workers cannot communicate with each other, but clients can. The producers are isolated as there is no connection between the supply side and the demand side. The project platform is designed to favor demand, while the network is controlled by the owners of the platform.

Under this regime of cognitive capitalism, which includes both aggregated and disaggregated distribution, use value creation expands exponentially but exchange value only rises linearly and is almost exclusively realized by capital, giving rise to forms of hyper-exploitation. We could call this value regime neo-feudal, because it often relies on unpaid 'corvée' (i.e., statute labor) and creates wide-spread debt peonage. Ownership is replaced by access, diminishing the sovereignty that comes with property, and creating dependencies through the one-sided licensing agreements in the digital sphere. We would argue that it creates a form of hyper-neoliberalism. While in classic neoliberalism labor income stagnates, in hyper-neoliberalism society is deproletarized, that is, wage labor is increasingly replaced by isolated and mostly precarious freelancers; more use value escapes the labor form altogether. Under the mixed regime of cognitive capi-talism in its netarchical form, networked value production grows, and has many emancipatory effects in the social field of use value creation. However, this is in contradiction with the field of exchange value realization, where hyper-exploitation occurs. In other words, there is an increased contradiction between the proto-mode of production, which is peer production, and associated forms of networked value

DOI: 10.1057/9781137406897.0010

creation with the relations of production, which remain under the domination of financial capital.

To sum up, we define 'netarchical capitalism' as the first combination (upper-left) which matches centralized control of a distributed infrastructure with an orientation toward the accumulation of capital. Netarchical capital is that fraction of capital which enables and empowers cooperation and P2P dynamics, but through proprietary platforms that are under central control. While individuals will share through these platforms, they have no control, governance or ownership over the design and the protocol of these networks/platforms, which are proprietary. Typically, under conditions of netarchical capitalism, sharers will directly create or share use value while the monetized exchange value will be realized by the owners of capital. Whereas in the short term it is in the interest of shareholders or owners, this also creates a longer-term value crisis for capital, since the value creators are not rewarded (or if they are, not in a decent way). They no longer have the purchasing power to acquire the goods that are necessary for the functioning of the physical economy.

On the one hand, in this technological regime a sector of capital has, to some significant degree, liberated itself of the need for proprietary forms of knowledge, but on the other, it has actually increased the level of surplus value extraction. At the same time, use value escapes more and more from its dependency on capital. This form of hyper-neoliberalism creates a crisis of value. The emergence of P2P models of production, based on the non-rivalrous nature and low marginal cost of digital information reproduction, coupled with the increasing unenforceability of IP laws, means that capital is incapable of realizing returns on ownership in the cognitive realm. In short, the creation of non-monetary value is exponential, whereas the monetization of such value is linear. There is a growing discrepancy between the direct creation of use value through social relationships and collective intelligence, but only a fraction of that value can actually be captured by business and money. Innovation is becoming social and diffuse; an emergent property of networks rather than an internal R&D affair within corporations. Hence, capital is becoming an a posteriori intervention in the realization of innovation rather than a condition for its occurrence, while more and more positive externalizations are created from the social field. What this announces is not only a crisis of value, most of which is 'beyond measure', but also essentially a crisis of accumulation of capital. Furthermore, we lack

DOI: 10.1057/9781137406897.0010

a mechanism for the existing institutional world to re-fund what it receives from the social world. On top of all of that, we have a crisis of social reproduction: peer production is collectively sustainable, but not individually (for an in-depth examination of these correlated issues, see Arvidsson and Pietersen, 2013).

DOI: 10.1057/9781137406897.0010

5
Distributed Capitalism

Abstract: *This chapter discusses the second technological regime/future scenario which develops within the context of a new-feudal form of cognitive capitalism. For Kostakis and Bauwens, 'distributed capitalism' matches distributed control over the infrastructure with a focus on capital accumulation. Under this technological regime, P2P infrastructures are designed in such a way as to allow the autonomy and participation of many players. Any Commons is a by-product or an afterthought of the system, and personal motivations are driven by exchange, trade and profit. Various P2P developments can be seen within this context, striving for a more inclusionary distributed and participative capitalism. Though they can be considered as part of an anti-systemic entrepreneurialism directed against the monopolies and predatory intermediaries, they retain the focus on profit making.*

Kostakis, Vasilis and Michel Bauwens. *Network Society and Future Scenarios for a Collaborative Economy.* Basingstoke: Palgrave Macmillan, 2014. DOI: 10.1057/9781137406897.0011.

DOI: 10.1057/9781137406897.0011

The second combination, (bottom-left) called 'distributed capitalism', matches distributed control over the back-end while maintaining a focus on capital accumulation. Under this technological regime, P2P infrastructures are designed in such a way as to allow the autonomy and participation of many players. Any Commons is a by-product or after-thought of the system, and personal motivations are driven by exchange, trade and profit. Various P2P developments can be seen within this context, striving for a more inclusionary, distributed and participative capitalism. Though they can be considered part of, say, an anti-systemic entrepreneurialism directed against monopolies and predatory inter-mediaries, they retain the focus on profit making. In the first scenario of netarchical capitalism, control and governance are located within a single proprietary hierarchy, whereas in distributed capitalism, control is located in the network of participating for-profit entrepreneurs and individuals. While netarchical capitalism mainly exploits human coop-eration, distributed capitalism is premised on the idea that everybody can trade and exchange; or, to put it bluntly, that 'everyone can become an independent capitalist'. Of course, as we already discussed, this idea could be central to a few netarchical projects as well, such as Airbnb and TaskRabbit, which enable the monetization of small players. However, their back-ends are not distributed as with distributed capitalist projects, or in other words, in the anarcho-capitalist/libertarian projects.

The libertarian political ideology, on which many projects from this quadrant are premised, advocates the elimination of the state in favor of individual sovereignty, private property and free/open markets (for a treatise of anarcho-capitalism, see Stringham, 2007). As the following analysis of well-known projects from this technological regime will show, the aforementioned ideology is illusionary. In theory you have equipotential individuals (i.e., everyone can potentially participate in a project), but in practice what one gets is concentrated capital and centralized governance. Moreover, we see the emergence of oligarchies and aristocracies. One could postulate that the anarcho-capitalist design of this technological regime, based on the Austrian school of econom-ics (see Schulak and Unterköfler, 2011), in many ways exacerbates the characteristics of the neoliberal era. As stated above, the P2P currency Bitcoin and the Kickstarter crowdfunding platform are representative examples of these developments.

To begin with, Bitcoin was first introduced in 2008 in a paper by Satoshi Nakamoto, which is presumed to be a pseudonym. It is basically

DOI: 10.1057/9781137406897.0011

a FLOSS (i.e., part of the Commons) that supports the movement of currencies. The software circumvents banks and enables the circulation of alternative currency by exploiting P2P networks. Instead of distributing the currency through a centralized network controlled by a central bank, Bitcoins are distributed by nodes participating in a P2P network (much like the BitTorrent file-sharing protocol). Further, as a FLOSS, the Bitcoin system can be monitored by all users worldwide, while participants in the development and improvement of its code cannot make changes that transcend the logic of its original design. Bitcoin is often viewed as an 'apolitical currency' (Varoufakis, 2013), devoid of the troubles that burden other currencies due to it simply being code which is controlled by no one. Yet this is not the case. Besides the fact that there are signs of emerging governance structures in Bitcoin, we can also see that its entire logic follows the key rules of other currencies. The code is in charge rather than the central banks, but as Lessig (2006) puts it, on the Internet the 'code is law', thus pointing out the politicalness imbued in each piece of software. In the real world, the law enables banks to mediate credit transactions between various parties. The law ensures the credibility of contracts, protects property rights and regulates money circulation (Lessig, 2006). Whereas in the digital world, according to Lessig (2006), the code assumes this role and defines what users can and cannot do. Therefore Bitcoin, as a piece of software, is imbued with ideas drawn from a certain political framework, as explained earlier. In other words, the P2P aspect of this project is actually not in the people, but in the computer and the code.

Moreover, Bitcoin is deliberately scarce. By limiting it to 24 million units, Nakamoto (or whoever is behind this project) has created a condition in which the more popular Bitcoin becomes, the higher its price gets. Of course, this makes it more and more difficult to use. The buyer will be motivated to stall any transactions to take advantage of the climbing price, while the seller, for instance an artisan, would buy material now and, by the time the final product is ready, the price would be unfavorable. In short, a deflationary currency puts pressure on the producer/seller to sell as fast as possible, while buyers prefer to wait in order to maximize their purchases. This situation clearly leads to crises. Presumably, the creators' intention was to create a currency free from debt, in the spirit of various politico-economical critiques against the credit system. Bitcoins do not come about as credit relations between two parties but rather as 'private' information in a network.

DOI: 10.1057/9781137406897.0011

The formulation of a Bitcoin 'aristocracy' is the result of the code's architecture. Members of this aristocracy are those that got into the Bitcoin game early on, when it was easy to create new units, as well as the owners of the so-called monster machines, powerful computers that specialize in Bitcoin mining (Davies, 2013). This small percentage of users have accumulated a great deal of Bitcoins, thus not only exhibiting features of the credit system it is supposed to be trying to overcome, but also threatening the viability of the whole project. Our thesis is that Bitcoin is not a Commons-oriented project aiming to satisfy the needs of society, rather a currency that inaugurates distributed capitalism. This new iteration of capitalism conforms to the characteristics of the network era and utilizes P2P infrastructures in order to achieve capital accumulation. Bitcoin is designed to allow multiple users, providing autonomy, but in a competitive framework. It might appear that it exists outside the financial system but, by promoting scarcity and competition, this project aggravates the overaccumulation of capital and exacerbates the social inequalities that it is supposed to combat.

Furthermore, Kickstarter is a crowdfunding platform which enables people to pledge money to provide the means for projects to happen. If the money is raised, the project is then funded, and the people who pledged get whatever they were promised. Kickstarter functions as a reverse market with prepaid investment. In other words, it can be seen as an extension of capitalism: instead of going to the banks for money, you go to the people. According to our four-scenario approach and depending on the point of view, Kickstarter could be considered a netarchical project as well. However, since the surplus value that is extracted here comes from the P2P financing of each project, and thus, the back-end coincides with the front-end (at least from the users' perspective), we place Kickstarter in the bottom-left quadrant, although quite near to the upper-left quadrant (Figure 5.1).

According to Bulajewski (2012), Kickstarter is actually a sophisticated web-hosting provider which charges '60 times the actual cost of providing a service by skimming a percentage off financial transactions'. In other words, Bulajewski (2012) concludes, '[Kickstarter] is the very definition of parasitic capitalism.' He is not the only one who considers Kickstarter as scam, pinpointing its exploitative nature. One could find hundreds of similar allegations and critiques online, but only a few scholarly papers on the topic. Setting these accusations aside, it remains a fact that Kickstarter is nothing more than a web-hosting provider with

DOI: 10.1057/9781137406897.0011

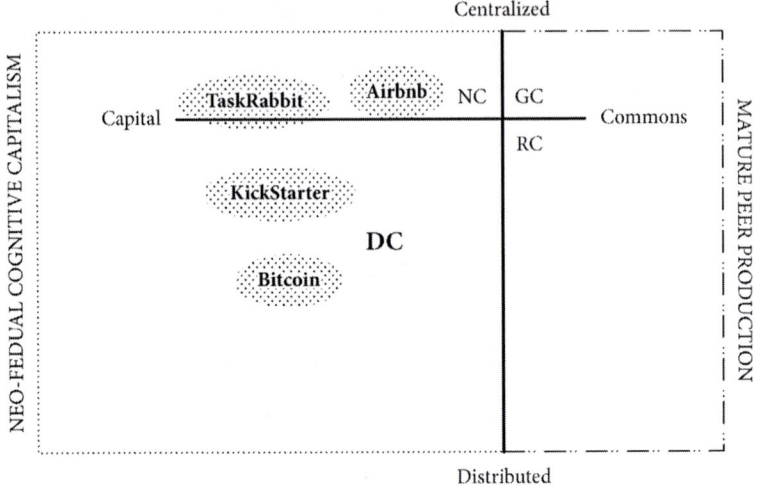

FIGURE 5.1   *The distributed capitalism quadrant*

an exchange platform and no community aspect, although it carries some interesting dynamics. This argument becomes more evident if we look at Kickstarter versus the community-oriented funding platform Goteo, whose projects must have a strong connection to the Commons. In the next part, we will address more projects such as Goteo, however, it is important first to highlight the progressive aspects, if any, of the cognitive capitalist projects that were already brought to the fore. This will be discussed in the following chapter.

DOI: 10.1057/9781137406897.0011

6

The Social Dynamics of the Mixed Model of Neo-feudal Cognitive Capitalism

Abstract: *This chapter highlights the progressive aspects of the cognitive capitalist projects that were discussed in the two previous chapters. The critical observation and documentation of the potentialities of such projects can arguably offer valuable lessons and chances for utilization. This chapter claims that Commons-based communities can benefit from capitalist platforms while struggling for their own rights as the real value creators and could potentially take over such platforms as common or publicly owned utilities. Moreover, they can fork and/or utilize best practices and technologies developed with a for-profit orientation.*

Kostakis, Vasilis and Michel Bauwens. *Network Society and Future Scenarios for a Collaborative Economy*. Basingstoke: Palgrave Macmillan, 2014. DOI: 10.1057/9781137406897.0012.

DOI: 10.1057/9781137406897.0012

We argued that the mixed model of neo-feudal cognitive capitalism, as described through the two scenarios/technological regimes of the left quadrants, creates some untenable contradictions, such as a crisis of value. Moreover, we saw that the two scenarios of the emerging value model of cognitive capitalism share two characteristics in principle: first, their main aim is profit-maximization; and second, whatever social goods or relations might be produced are subsumed to the profit model. Hence, it becomes necessary to imagine a transition to a model where the relations of production will not be in contradiction with the evolution of the mode of production and the orientation will rest on the Commons. However, we realize that many forms of the first two scenarios are hybrid because they also allow the further growth of P2P sociality, in which media exchange and production are widely available to an ever-larger user base. For instance, platforms such as Facebook, YouTube or Twitter could become a social utility. The instrumental role of proprietary social media in the success of, for example, the Egyptian anti-government protests which led to the resignation of Egypt's dictatorial leader is almost unquestionable (Eltantawy and Wiest, 2011; Khamis and Vaughn, 2011; Vargas, 2012). Or imagine a YouTube owned by filmmakers and cinemas, and an Amazon owned by authors and independent bookshops. Therefore, there are netarchical platforms that build P2P infrastructures and create some positive conditions which should be critically utilized for a more autonomous network society. Another example is IBM and its coalition with various Commons-based projects in the realm of software. As already postulated, IBM profits on the use value produced through peer production processes. Nevertheless, its involvement has catalyzed the enhancement of the outputs and contributed to the sustainability of many Commons-based projects offering chances for paid labor.

In addition, moving to the distributed capitalism scenario, Bitcoin is extremely important as a signpost, since it is the first global 'post-Westphalian' currency based on 'social sovereignty'. It actually shows that alternative currencies could scale and exist as a workable alternative. Bitcoin, whether it will fail to meet its ambitious goals or not, has paved the way for a new type of currency that utilizes new technological infrastructures, and whose dynamics should not be ignored. As discussed, Bitcoin's protocol enables a decentralized network to achieve consensus, without requiring any trust between parties. Also, the potential of its innovations (e.g., the blockchain) is so big that it has caught the attention of major banking institutions. However, we would say that the most

DOI: 10.1057/9781137406897.0012

important achievement is that it envisions an alternative approach to tackling the major problems in the current credit system. As an open source software program, Bitcoin can get upgraded and it can also get forked. We are witnessing a plethora of new digital currencies based on Bitcoin which aim to surpass some of the issues that were discussed in the previous chapter. Their efforts revolve around the belief that the current financial system is based on an unsustainable principle of continuous growth, and attempt to implement social values into their structure. Openmoney and the OpenUDC are indicative of such efforts. Both projects provide the opportunity for communities to create their own alternative currencies. Peercoin, on the other hand, functions similarly to Bitcoin, but attempts to overcome its problems. Some of these currencies are based on the trust between members of a community of producers and consumers, while others allow mathematics to eliminate the concept of interest from the core of the financial system. Furthermore, crowdfunding platforms, such as Kickstarter, have sometimes enabled the funding and the development of novel, Commons-oriented projects. For example, at the time of this writing (March 2014), more than 220 projects have been tagged as open source and a considerable number of those have been successfully funded, according to the Kickstarter (2014) website.

The critical observation and documentation of the potentialities of projects placed in the two left quadrants can offer valuable lessons and opportunities for utilization. Commons-based communities can benefit from capitalist platforms while struggling for their own rights as the real value creators and, in conditions of social strength, could potentially take over such platforms as common or publicly owned utilities. Moreover, they can fork and/or utilize best practices (e.g., the case of Goteo in relation to Kickstarter) and technologies (e.g., the Bitcoin protocol) developed with a for-profit orientation. We propose that this can happen through the creation of non-capitalist, community-supportive, benefit-driven entities that participate in market exchange without participating in capital accumulation. Before articulating some preliminary policy proposals for such a working hypothesis, we should discuss the next two scenarios/technological regimes based on a different orientation, that of building, empowering and protecting the Commons sphere.

DOI: 10.1057/9781137406897.0012

Part III

The Hypothetical Model of Mature Peer Production: Toward a Commons-Oriented Economy and Society

▶ Plenty of attention has been gathering around the Commons (see Ostrom, 1990; Hardt and Negri, 2011; Barnes, 2006; Benkler, 2006; Bollier and Helfrich, 2012). But what is its concept all about? As we will discuss below, echoing Bollier (2014), the Commons might simultaneously refer to shared resources, a discourse, a new/old property framework, social processes, an ethic, a set of policies or, in other words, to a paradigm of a pragmatic new societal vision beyond the dominant capitalist system. To begin with, in general Commons refers to shared resources where each stakeholder has an equal interest (Ostrom, 1990). The Commons sphere can include natural gifts such as air, water, the oceans and wildlife, and shared 'assets' or creative work such as the Internet, the airwaves, the languages, our cultural heritage and public knowledge which have been accumulating since time immemorial (Bollier, 2002, 2005, 2009). The Commons, with a capital 'C' to highlight its (re)emergence as a powerful counterweight to government and corporate power, also includes goods that have been developed and maintained jointly by a community (Siefkes, 2012; Mackinnon, 2012). These

DOI: 10.1057/9781137406897.0013

goods are shared according to certain community-defined rules (Siefkes, 2012). Take, for example, the Wikipedia encyclopedia or FLOSS, with regard to certain community-driven governance mechanisms through which these projects have managed to remain sustainable, functional and productive. Therefore, it could be said that every Commons scheme basically has four interlinked components: a resource (material and/or immaterial; replenishable and/or depletable); the community which shares it (the users, administrators, producers and/or providers); the use value created through the social reproduction or preservation of these common goods; and the rules and the participatory property regimes that govern people's access to it. There is an interplay among the aforementioned components and, therefore, as we discuss below, Commons should mostly be viewed as social processes.

In contrast to the traditional understanding of property, a key characteristic of the Commons is that no one has exclusive control over the use and disposition of any particular resource (Benkler, 2006). Unlike most things in modern capitalist society, the Commons is neither private nor public, in the traditional sense (The Ecologist, 1994, p. 109). The Commons may signify the absence of state, corporate and/or individual control, in favor of distributed control based upon non-exclusionary, P2P property regimes (Boyle, 2003a, 2003b; Bauwens, 2005). It would be interesting, here, to address the relation between the definitions of the public domain and the Commons. Both concepts are often used interchangeably, yet the latter seems to overtake the former in terms of popularity (Boyle, 2003a, 2003b). The public domain concept is related to the 'outside' of the IP system; it entails items free of property rights, and, thus, emphasizes totally open accessibility: nobody is excluded and everything is allowed (Boyle, 2003a). On the other side, the Commons can be restrictive in a sense. For instance, some Commons-based projects give the freedom to use and/or modify the resource under the condition that new contributions will also be open to others under the same conditions. Hence, the Commons is not an ungoverned space but rather a legal regime for ensuring that the artifacts of community-based productive efforts remain under the control of that community: 'The GPL, the CC licenses, databases of traditional knowledge, and sui generis national statutes for protecting biological diversity all represent innovative legal strategies for protecting the commons' (Bollier, 2009, p. 219). Therefore, we may consider the public domain as a container in which the Commons represents its content of jointly held resources (Ciffolilli,

2004). When Hardin was discussing the tragedy of the Commons in his 1968 essay, he was actually describing a regime free of property rights and/or of governance mechanisms, where everybody could take and use anything with no constraint. However, in the Commons, a distinct community of users governs the resource (Bollier, 2014, p. 3). Hardin's thesis has also been called 'The Tragedy of Unmanaged, Laissez-Faire, Common-Pool Resources with Easy-Access for Non-Communicating, Self-Interest Individuals' (Hyde, 2010, p. 44). We do not argue that humans are not self-interested and competitive beings, but that they simultaneously exhibit deep concern for fairness, communication, reciprocity, solidarity and social connection: 'all these human traits', Bollier (2014, p. 3) writes, 'lie at the heart of the commons'. Benkler (2011) brings empirical evidence to the fore and describes how cooperation in Commons-based projects triumphs over self-interest, making a case against the blind adherence to 'free market' dogmas.

On the one hand, the neoliberal economics have integrated both the state and the market into one organism/entity, the 'market/state', which stresses the 'deep interdependencies among large corporations, political leaders, and government bodies' (Bollier, 2014, p. 1). The market/state rarely takes into consideration any 'positive' human trait when designing and implementing public policies. Rather, it sees competition, individualism and private property as key drivers of growth and innovation. A critique against neoliberalism could be that it systematizes only a very limited aspect of complex human nature. In contrast, the P2P-driven, Commons-oriented social systems are designed not for one motivation (rational self-interest), but for a multitude of motivations (it is motivation-agnostic). No matter how 'selfish' is the motivation of the Linux or Wikipedia contributors, the system is designed to ensure that participating individuals contribute to the Commons. In the narrow sense, it could be said that the P2P-driven, Commons-based production efforts encapsulate complex human behavior so that it can contribute to the creation of Commons.

Moreover, the mainstream economic theory and many of its prominent indexes (such the Global National Product, GDP) are incapable of recognizing the value produced through various Commons-based projects. Typically, the Commons-oriented forms of production do not produce commodities, but rather use value, and, thus, the latter is not treated as property (The Ecologist, 1994). Hence, the Commons is not recognized as having economic value and cannot take part in

DOI: 10.1057/9781137406897.0013

market exchange within its social/collective/non-exclusive format (Brown, 2010). To tackle this problem, the capitalist political economy would treat the shared resource as a commodity. Enclosed by a certain exclusive property regime – property is a political institution, as Brown (2010) points out – the resource can now enter the market and become a means for profit maximization. According to this perspective, wealth is synonymous with the accumulation of properties; therefore, everything has to be commodified, even things that are more than commodities:

> Labor is only another name for a human activity which goes with life itself, which in its turn is not produced for sale but for entirely different reasons, nor can that activity be detached from the rest of life, be stored or mobilized; land is only another name for nature, which is not produced by man; actual money, finally, is merely a token of purchasing power which, as a rule, is not produced at all, but comes into being through the mechanism of banking or state finance. None of them is produced for sale. The commodity description of labor, land, and money is entirely fictitious. (Polanyi, 1944/2001, pp. 75–76)

From the parliamentary enclosures in England (15th–19th centuries) to the recent 'corporate enclosures', a vast range of commonly held resources has been enclosed, privatized, traded in the market, and thus abused (Bollier, 2002; McCann, 2012). The first wave of enclosure forced people who had been making their living outside the wage mechanism to leave their lands for the cities, where they began to be dependent on wages for their survival (Brown, 2010). They became workers, cogs of the capitalist mode of production. If we follow Marx (1992/1885, 1993/1973), this was an alienation of the self from itself, because what workers produced was very divorced from who they were, thus damaging their essential integrity. And as Brown (2010, p. 120) remarks: 'the alienation of labor caused by an economics of property has repeated itself with a vengeance in our relationship with the living planet.'

However, in the second wave of enclosure, taking place nowadays, there is a robust counter-power: the distributed movement of the Commons with a local and global orientation. There are areas where the market is retreating, not to the bureaucracies and command structures, but instead to the Commons (Stadler, 2014): from seed-sharing cooperatives, the FLOSS and open hardware communities, to localities that use alternative currencies, resilient communities and movements such as community-supported agriculture and Transition Towns. We are observing a re-emergence and flowering of new economic forms based

DOI: 10.1057/9781137406897.0013

on equity, including the cooperative economy, the social economy and the solidarity economy. The reduction of transaction and coordination costs through the modern ICT and the distribution of productive capital in the form of networked personal computers have strengthened this current and given birth to new forms of production based on the collaborative efforts of autonomous individuals. These collaborative modes of social production, which principally celebrate open access to knowledge, have mainly been labeled 'Commons-based peer production' (see Benkler, 2006, 2011; Bauwens, 2005, 2009). The first Commons-based peer production (CBPP) projects were observed in the sphere of information economy, where the marginal cost of information production is very low, if not nearly zero (Benkler, 2006; Bauwens, 2005; Rifkin, 2014; Kostakis, 2012). A plethora of projects, such as the development of the Linux Kernel, the Apache Web server, the office suite LibreOffice, the browser Mozilla Firefox, and the operating system Ubuntu, and free/open content projects such as the encyclopedia Wikipedia, exemplify the productive and governance processes of CBPP. Moreover, we have observed similar patterns of production in some emerging or even not-so-new Commons-based, P2P projects in the primary and secondary economic sector.

As a first example, the Centre for Sustainable Agriculture in India is a community-managed agriculture model that focuses on developing and promoting locally adapted and sustainable farming systems. It was developed to provide a viable alternative for Indian farmers who were being crushed by the cost of chemical pesticides, fertilizers and genetically modified seeds. Open source seed-sharing networks and community seed banks have been set up to overcome the various IP limitations that turned seeds, traditionally considered a Commons, into objects of exclusionary property (Dafermos, 2014). These efforts aim to create a knowledge database (an agricultural Commons, one might say) for the conservation and revival of existing varieties as well as for practices of participatory plant breeding on a local basis (Aoki, 2009; Kloppenburg, 2010; Raidu and Ramanjaneyulu, 2008). Moreover, several producer-consumer cooperatives have been set up with their own meeting grounds (Dafermos, 2014). Another P2P project that goes beyond the information sphere of production is the Transition Towns movement, a grassroots network of communities that is working to build resilience in response to peak oil, climate destruction, and economic instability. Its approach is based on 'a concisely crafted methodology for catalyzing community participation via a messy open source organizational process' (Robb, 2009). Likewise, the Open Source Ecology project concerns the development of several low-cost machines meant to cover all sorts of agricultural, and even manufacturing, needs. The design information for these machines is globally available under Commons-oriented licenses adapted for hardware. Another initiative of great interest is the RepRap project, which initially included the development of a low-cost open source 3D printer that could replicate itself by printing a number of its own components. Its lack of IP restrictions has enabled a huge community to experiment with, and improve on, the design. As a result, several models based on the first RepRap model have recently been developed. In addition, not only multiple start-ups but also some large companies began making low-cost 3D printers based on the RepRap design. Another example of CBPP efforts in the manufacturing sector would be the Wikispeed project. Its aim is to produce an energy efficient and modular car made at a fraction of the price of a conventional car. Developed by an international community of volunteers, the Wikispeed car can be built on demand in micro-factories with the use of free/open source software and hardware. Anyone can use or contribute to the project, as all of the specifications are available.

Under the lens of a processual vision of social change (Papadopoulos, Stephenson and Tsianos, 2008), these socially driven projects could be considered as escape routes to alternative forms of social organization. If the political agenda for a world driven by social-oriented values should include the removal of property relations as the economy's foundation and their replacement with civic relation, or, access to resources over ownership (Brown, 2010), then the Commons-oriented movement seems to be emblematic of the aforementioned approach. IP rights are reconfigured to prevent the monetization and expropriation of knowledge. New institutionalized licenses have been introduced to allow the unobstructed sharing of information, including the Creative Commons licenses, the General Public Licenses (GPL) or the Peer Production Licenses (PPL). These forms of property allow the social reproduction of Commons-oriented projects. In other words, knowledge is considered a common good and becomes available to anyone through the utilization of the Internet. Thus, experimentation, collaborative innovation and development are truly promoted while remaining community-driven (Moglen, 2004; Wendel de Joode, 2005; Benkler, 2006).

DOI: 10.1057/9781137406897.0013

However, the aforementioned projects, which form what we could call 'the hypothetical model of mature peer production under civic dominance' (right quadrants), may differ in their focus on the Commons as either local or global. We use the term 'local' as a space distinct from the larger regional, national and international spaces (Sharzer, 2012). In addition, local can be also relational, seen as a moment in the global capital accumulation (ibid.). On the other side, the use of the term 'global' recognizes the possibility that a project might be local, but with the meaning of a spatial territory. This is to say, a project can be rooted somewhere, but the produced use value is principally aimed at a global audience. Our main idea is that networks are global-local, thus, for-benefit orientations can either focus on pure relocalization strategies (though they can be globally organized to achieve this), or they can take a global perspective and create global Commons through global for-benefit associations and global entrepreneurial coalitions. In the 'resilient communities' (RC) scenario (bottom-right) there is distributed control over the P2P infrastructures, that is, both the back-end and the front-end are solely distributed. The focus here is mostly on relocalization and the re-creation of local communities. It is often based on an expectation of a future marked by severe shortages or, in any case, increased scarcity of energy and resources, and so takes the form of lifeboat strategies. Initiatives such as the Transition Towns movement, the degrowth movement or certain aspects of the India-based CSA can be seen in that context. The 'Global Commons' (GC) approach (upper-right) is in contrast to the aforementioned focus on the local, focusing instead on the global Commons. Advocates and builders of this scenario argue that the Commons should be created and fought for on a transnational global scale. The necessity to scale up the Commons is evident in this particular scenario. As becomes obvious, contrary to the left quadrants we do not deal here in terms of technological regimes. Instead, we are more interested in the orientation that communities and individuals have when utilizing P2P infrastructures. The following chapters discuss separately and in more detail each scenario, concluding with some transition proposals for moving toward a global Commons-oriented economy, which arguably can take full advantage of the current TEP's potential in a more sustainable and just way.

DOI: 10.1057/9781137406897.0013

7
Resilient Communities

Abstract: *This chapter addresses the third future scenario which has a local orientation with a focus on the Commons. In the 'resilient communities' scenario there is distributed control over the P2P infrastructures while the focus is mostly on relocalization and the re-creation of local communities. It is often based on an expectation for a future marked by severe shortages of energy and resources, and it often takes the form of lifeboat strategies. However, the resilient communities do not build global structures when the issue, according to Kostakis and Bauwens, is how to organize a global counter-power that can propose alternative modes of social organization on a global scale.*

Kostakis, Vasilis and Michel Bauwens. *Network Society and Future Scenarios for a Collaborative Economy*. Basingstoke: Palgrave Macmillan, 2014. DOI: 10.1057/9781137406897.0014.

The primarily ecological and subsequently economic, social, cultural and political crises the world is facing is the point of departure for the resilient communities approach. This scenario contains strategies and policies for strengthening the ability to adapt to such uneven changes. It makes the case for a transition to a low-carbon, sustainable sharing economy based on social justice and cooperative interactions between people, where economic growth is out of the picture (Lewis and Conaty, 2012). For instance, the degrowth movement along with the Transition Towns, the car sharing and the general permaculture movements can be seen in this context (Figure 7.1).

The theoretical bedrock of the degrowth movement is the so-called degrowth economics, associated with the work of Latouche (2009). According to this body of thought, a radical shift has to take place from growth as the main objective of the modern economy toward its opposite, that is, contraction and downshifting (Foster, 2011; Latouche, 2009). Latouche's work has since given rise to new intellectual movements and inspired a revival of radical Green thought, especially in Europe, as manifested by some prominent conferences in Paris (2008) and Barcelona (2010) (Foster, 2011). The Transition Towns movement, among others, has been influenced by the ideas of degrowth economics. The goal here is the radical relocalization of politics, economics

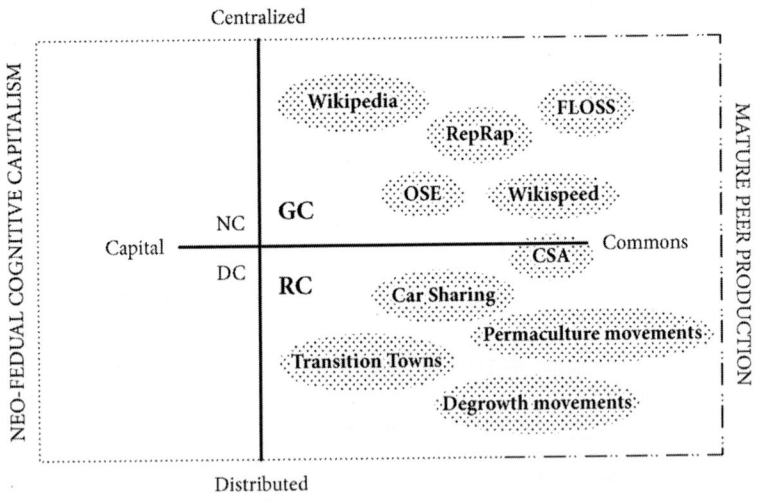

FIGURE 7.1   *The Commons-oriented quadrants*

DOI: 10.1057/9781137406897.0014

and culture to autonomous and self-sufficient communities, in order to become resilient to mega changes, such as peak oil and climate change. Hopkins – who, in 2006, created a working model of a Transition Town community in Totnes, UK – first introduced this concept in his 2008 book *The Transition Handbook*. Since then there have been over a hundred networked transition communities in existence or in the planning stages (see Chamberlin, 2009; Hopkins, 2011). Such communities are of a size that would allow members to have a strong personal influence over collective decisions (Hopkins, 2008, 2011). The Transition Towns concept has as its bedrock not only open source organizational practices, but also the principles of permaculture in combination with resilience and relocalization. Permaculture, a term which stands for 'permanent agriculture', is the design and maintenance of agricultural ecosystems which have the diversity, stability and resilience of natural ecosystems (Mollison, 1988). As Mollison (1988, p. ix–x) puts it:

> The philosophy behind permaculture is one of working with, rather than against nature; of protracted and thoughtful observation rather than protracted and thoughtless action; of looking at systems in all their functions rather than asking only one yield of them; and of allowing systems to demonstrate their own evolutions.

A system based on permaculture principles and practices can evolve, self-organize and thereby survive almost any change: there is no insistence on a single culture, which would shut down learning and cut back resilience (Meadows, 2008, p. 160). Hence, in order to counter the volatility and fragility of the dominant system, building resilience locally is fundamental (Lewis and Conaty, 2012). It is vital to shift to a system with the capacity 'to evolve without losing its core sense of identity or purpose' (Wilding, 2011, p. 19). Therefore, resilience can be seen as the degree to which the system is capable of learning, self-organizing and adapting while remaining coherent (Carpenter et al., 2001; Walker et al., 2009; Folke, 2006). Walker and Salt (2006) along with Lewis and Conaty (2012) highlight some key aspects of any system's resilience: diversity, modularity (consisting of components which can independently operate and be modified), reciprocity, social capital (i.e., trust and bond among members) and tightness of feedback loops. In general:

> [A] system's resilience is enhanced by more diversity and more connections, because there are more channels to fall back on in times of trouble or change. Efficiency, on the other hand, increases through streamlining,

DOI: 10.1057/9781137406897.0014

which usually means reducing diversity and connectivity... Because both are indispensable for long-term sustainability and health, the healthiest flow systems are those that maintain an optimal balance between these two opposing pulls. (Walker and Salt, 2006, p. 121)

Steps and policies toward the world that the resilient communities' scenario envisions can be: the support of a dynamic local economy; the empowerment of local governance and local control; the optimization of assets; the valuing of local distinctiveness and of permaculture; the development of sustainable infrastructures (e.g., affordable housing; interest-free banks; community land trusts; autonomous energy production etc.); and the construction of a social solidarity economy (Wilding, 2011; Lewis and Conaty, 2012).

The local focus of the resilient communities quadrant becomes, however, evident. In extreme forms, this scenario contains simple lifeboat strategies and initiatives, aimed at the survival of small communities in the context of generalized chaos. They may build on the idea that we must accept the reality of considerably more expensive energy and food (Lewis and Conaty, 2012). What marks some of these initiatives is arguably the abandonment of the ambition of scale while the feudalization of territorial integrity is considered mostly inevitable. Though global cooperation and web presence may exist, the focus remains on the local. Most often, political and social mobilization at scale is seen as not realistic, and doomed to failure. In the context of our profit making versus Commons axis though, these projects are squarely aimed at generating community value. We consider them a healthy reaction against global problems and environmental degradation.

Resilient communities try to be immune to the dominant system and they use P2P practices and technologies for good reasons. They try to support individuals' physical and psychological well-being by generating a positive sense of place, localizing the economy within ecological limits and securing entrepreneurial/community stewardship of the local Commons (Wilding, 2011). They do not, however, build global structures. According to our understanding, the issue is how to organize a global counter-power able to propose alternative modes of social organization on a global scale. For Sharzer (2012), 'localism' is the fetishization of scale, as some positive benefit is ascribed to a place precisely because it is small. He argues that resilient communities and other similar projects inevitably become parts of the broader capitalist economy, because they do not confront capitalism, but rather avoid it. Initiatives such as

DOI: 10.1057/9781137406897.0014

Transition Towns are growing movements, though with local focus. They can coexist in harmony within the next scenario of global Commons by the logic that whatever is heavy is local (e.g., desktop manufacturing technologies), and whatever is light is global (e.g., global knowledge Commons).

In addition to the focus on the local, the degrowth narrative is central to the resilient communities scenario. We believe, quoting Foster (2011), 'that the ecological struggle, understood in these terms, must aim not merely for degrowth in the abstract but more concretely for de-accumulation – a transition away from a system geared to the accumulation of capital without end'. To realize such a transition it is crucial to develop pragmatic alternatives. Similar to how we began talking about 'alter-globalization' when the 'antiglobalization' movement became counter-intuitive, we now need to become more positive and start talking about 'alter-growth' scenarios instead of thinking in anti-growth/degrowth terms. Arguably, the issue is not to produce and consume less per se, but to develop new models of production which will work on a higher level than capitalist models. We consider it difficult to challenge the dominant system if we lack a working plan to transcend it. A post-capitalist world is bound to entail more than a mere reversal to pre-industrial times. As the TEPS theory informs us, the adaptation of current institutions and the creation of new ones take place in the deployment phase of each TEP. We claim that the times are, finally, mature enough to introduce a radical political agenda with brand new institutions, fueled by the spirit of the Commons and aiming to provide a viable global alternative to the capitalist paradigm beyond degrowth or antiglobalization rhetorics.

DOI: 10.1057/9781137406897.0014

8

Global Commons

Abstract: *This chapter deals with the 'Global Commons' scenario which celebrates the hypothetical model of mature peer production. Advocates of this scenario argue that the Commons should be created and fought for on a global scale. Though production is distributed and therefore facilitated at the local level, the resulting micro-factories are considered as essentially networked on a global scale, profiting from the mutualized global cooperation both on the design of the product, and on the improvement of the common machinery. Political and social mobilization, on regional, national and transnational scale, is seen as part of the struggle for the transformation of institutions. According to Kostakis and Bauwens, this scenario does not take social regression as given, and believes in sustainable abundance for the whole of humanity.*

Kostakis, Vasilis and Michel Bauwens. *Network Society and Future Scenarios for a Collaborative Economy*. Basingstoke: Palgrave Macmillan, 2014. DOI: 10.1057/9781137406897.0015.

DOI: 10.1057/9781137406897.0015

Several global-oriented Commons-based projects such as FLOSS, Wikipedia, Wikispeed, RepRap or Open Source Ecology (OSE) highlight the emergence of technological capabilities shaped by human factors, which in turn shape the environment in which humans live and work. They create what Benkler (2006, p. 31) calls new 'technological-economic feasibility spaces' for social practice. These feasibility spaces include different social and economic arrangements, where profit, power and control do not seem as predominant as they have in the history of modern capitalism. From this new communicational, interconnected, virtual environment, a new social productive model is emerging, different from the industrial one. We are witnessing the emergence of a new proto-mode of production, that is, Commons-based peer production, based on distributed, collaborative forms of organization. It is developing within capitalism, rather as Marx (1979) argued that the early forms of merchant and factory capitalism developed within the feudal order. In other words, system change is back on the agenda, but in an unexpected form, not as a 'socialist' alternative, but as a Commons-based alternative. As we saw, capitalism in its present form is facing limits, especially resource limits, and in spite of the rapid growth of the BRICS (Brazil, Russia, India, China and South Africa) economies, it is undergoing a process of decomposition. The question is whether the new proto-mode can generate the institutional capacity and alliances needed to break the political power of the old order. Ultimately, the potential of the new mode is the same as those of previous proto-modes of production – to emancipate itself from dependency on the old decaying mode, to become self-sustaining and thus replace the accumulation of capital with the circulation of the Commons. In an independent circulation of the Commons, the common use value would directly contribute to the further strengthening of the Commons and of the commoners' own sustainability, without dependence on capital. How could this be achieved? Before dealing with this tempting question, we believe that it is crucial to shed more light on the social, economic and political dynamics of CBPP.

When it comes to information, CBPP is more productive than market-based or the 'bureaucratic-state' systems (Benkler, 2006). It produces social well-being because it is based on people's intrinsic positive motivations (i.e., the need to create, learn and communicate) and synergetic cooperation among participants and users (Benkler 2006; Hertel, Niedner, and Herrmann, 2003; Lakhani and Wolf, 2005). As

DOI: 10.1057/9781137406897.0015

Hertel, Niedner and Herrmann (2003, p. 1174) mention in their study of the incentives of 141 Linux kernel community participants, the latter were driven 'by similar motives as voluntary action within social movements such as the civil rights movement, the labor movement, or the peace movement'. Benkler (2006) makes two intriguing economic observations which challenge some 'eternal truths' of the mainstream economic theory. Commons-based projects fundamentally challenge the assumption that in economic production, the human being solely seeks profit maximization. Volunteers contribute to information production projects, while they gain knowledge, experience and reputation, and communicate with each other motivated by intrinsically positive incentives. This does not mean that the monetary motive is totally absent; however, it is relegated to a peripheral concept (Benkler, 2006). The second challenge is directed against the conventional wisdom that, in Benkler's (2006, p. 463) words, 'we have only two basic free transactional forms – property-based markets and hierarchically organized firms.' CBPP can be considered a third way, and should not be treated as an exception but rather as a widespread phenomenon, although it is not currently counted in the economic census (Benkler, 2006). In terms of neoliberal economics, what is happening in CBPP can arguably be considered only in the sense that individuals are free to contribute, or take what they need, following their individual inclinations, with an invisible hand bringing it all together yet without any monetary mechanism. Hence, in contrast to markets, in CBPP the allocation of resources is not done through a market-pricing mechanism. Hybrid modes of governance are employed, and what is generated is not profit, but a Commons.

CBPP is based on practices that stand in contrast to those of the market-based business firms. More specifically, CBPP is opposed to industrial firms' hierarchical control and authority. Instead, it is based on communal validation and negotiated coordination (see, for instance, Dafermos' (2012) study on the Free BSD project's collectivist and consensus-oriented governance system) as quality control is community-driven, and conflicts are solved through an ongoing mediated dialogue (e.g., in Wikipedia, the dialogue takes place in the discussion page of each article). However, in cases such as the internal battle between inclusionists and deletionists, Wikipedia's lack of a clearly defined constitution led a small number of participants to create rules in conflict with others: persistent, well-organized minorities adroitly handled their opponents,

DOI: 10.1057/9781137406897.0015

seriously challenging the sustainability of the project (Kostakis, 2010). Therefore, it must be stressed that when abundance is replaced by scarcity (as happened in Wikipedia when deletionists demanded strict content control), power structures emerge because CBPP mechanisms cannot function well (Kostakis, 2010). Investigating prominent CBPP projects, O'Neil (2009) analyzed the tensions generated by the distribution of authority, and showed that it is important to discuss openly how power and authority actually work in CBPP in order to be able to organize differently. His proposal is that leaders must support maximum autonomy for participants toward a more egalitarian situation. Of course, a special characteristic of CBPP is that if these benevolent dictators (Kostakis, 2010) abuse their power, their leadership becomes malicious, and a substantial exodus of community members often occurs. These members, due to the low marginal costs of information, are free to start their own new project, using the already Commons-based peer-produced information if they wish.

Further, CBPP is not driven by the for-profit orientation that defines market projects, as peer projects have a for-benefit orientation, creating use value for their communities. This does not mean that the profit motive is totally absent in CBPP projects, but rather that incentives such as learning, communication and experience come to the fore. That is how the human person actually operates, rather than the imagined homo economicus. Besides, Hess' (2005, p. 515) 'private-sector symbiosis' hypothesis outlines that emphasis on technology and product innovation can lead 'to the articulation of social movements goals with those of inventors, entrepreneurs, and industrial reformers' (2005, p. 516). Therefore, 'a cooperative relationship emerges between advocacy organizations that support the alternative technologies/products, and private sector firms that develop and market alternative technologies' (ibid.). For instance, Linux and IBM come in accordance with Hess' argument for the private-sector symbiosis and subsequent incorporation and transformation of the technologies which may, though, provoke, an object conflict. 'As the technological/product field undergoes diversification', Hess (2005, p. 515) writes, object conflicts 'erupt over a range of design possibilities, from those advocated by the more social movement-oriented organizations to those advocated by the established industries'. It can be claimed that an object conflict is taking place concerning the Makerbot Replicator 2 3D printer, which is partly closed source. This may, arguably, lead to the loss of Makerbot's community (Giseburt, 2012).

DOI: 10.1057/9781137406897.0015

Instead of the division of labor in CBPP, a distribution of modular tasks takes place, with anyone able to contribute to any module, while the threshold for participation is as low as possible (see Benkler, 2006; Bauwens, 2005; Tapscott and Williams, 2006; Dafermos and Söderberg, 2009). Modularity is a key condition for CBPP to emerge: 'Described in technical terms, modularity is a form of task decomposition. It is used to separate the work of different groups of developers, creating, in effect, related yet separate sub-projects' (Dafermos and Söderberg, 2009, p. 61). Torvalds (1999), the instigator of the Linux project, maintains that the Linux kernel development model requires modularity, because in that way, people can work in parallel. Empirical research (see MacCormack, Rusnak and Baldwinet, 2007; Dafermos, 2012) shows that modular design is characteristic not just of Linux but of the FLOSS development model in general. According to Carson (2010, p. 208) 'The Unix philosophy of providing lots of small specialized tools that can be combined in versatile ways is probably the oldest expression in software of this modular style.' We also observe the same approach in the development of one of the most prominent CBPP projects, namely Wikipedia. Articles (i.e., modules), which consist of sections (or, sub-modules), are built upon other articles and entries produced, and thus can be used individually as well as in combination. By breaking up the raw elements into smaller modules, there is both an abundance of options in terms of remixing them, as well as a low participation threshold, since the individuals can have access to the modules rather than centralized forms of capital. Further, modularity leads to stigmergic collaboration. In its most generic formulation, according to Marsh and Onof (2007, p. 1), 'stigmergy is the phenomenon of indirect communication mediated by modifications of the environment.' Therefore, in the context of CBPP, stigmergic collaboration is the 'collective, distributed action in which social negotiation is stigmergically mediated by Internet-based technologies' (Elliott, 2006).

Moreover, CBPP is opposed to the rivalry (scarcity of goods) through which market profit is generated, as sharing the created goods does not diminish the value of the good, but actually enhances it (Benkler, 2006). To this, one might add that CBPP is facilitated by free, unconstrained and creative cooperation of communities, which lowers the legal restrictive barriers to such a process and invents new, institutionalized ways of sharing. In terms of property, as we have discussed, the Commons is an idea different both from state property, where the state manages a certain resource on behalf of the people, and from private property, where

DOI: 10.1057/9781137406897.0015

a private entity excludes the common use of it. It is, however, important to highlight that the contributors of CBPP projects do have interests and rights concerning their work and are interested in protecting their intellectual property (O'Mahony, 2003). Thus, the Commons-oriented approach to property 'does not assert that sharing is an ethical absolute' (after all everyone is, or should be, free to choose what type of license they will adopt), but tries to balance the rights of innovators with the rights of the public (O'Mahony, 2003; von Hippel and von Krogh, 2003). It becomes obvious that what sets CBPP apart from the proprietary-based mode of production – the 'industrial one' (Benkler, 2006) – is its modes of governance (consensus-oriented governance mechanisms) and property (communal shareholding), whose foundation stones are the abundance of resources, openness and the power of meaningful human cooperation. These are the very characteristics of CBPP which provide the capacity to deliver genuinely innovative, remarkable results (thus contesting allegations of low quality: see Keen, 2007; Lanier, 2010) such as the Apache web server, Mozilla Firefox browser, Linux kernel, BIND (the most widely used DNS software), Sendmail (router of the majority of e-mail) and a myriad of emerging open source hardware projects.

Of course, beyond the great potential of CBPP, there may well be numerous obstacles, theoretical and practical problems, and negative side effects. However, taken in this idealized context, CBPP arguably carries some aspects which create a political economy where economic efficiency, profit and competitiveness cease to be the sole guiding stars (Moore and Karatzogianni, 2009), while civil society attains a more important role, bringing (back) the notion of the Commons into the heart of the economy (Orsi, 2009). Under these lenses, the Commons can be seen as a legitimate vehicle of citizenship or as an equivalent of Tocqueville's (2010) civil society, through which citizens mobilize and express their interests while protecting their rights (Mackinnon, 2012). It can be central to the process of civilizing the economy, which would require a strong notion of citizenship – of membership in a global civil society (Brown, 2010). The Commons movement is removing property relations as our political economy's foundation and is replacing them with civic relations that define our bonds with each other – at work, in neighborhoods, in cities and in global communities (ibid.). The Commons is long-term social and material processes that cannot be created overnight: 'in order to become meaningful they must exist over an extensive period of time' (Stadler, 2014, p. 31). In other words, the

DOI: 10.1057/9781137406897.0015

various spheres of the Commons are products of P2P creative processes as they expand horizontally and in dense interconnections with each other. Therefore, we must go beyond a material understanding of the concept and approach the Commons not only as a resource or as a property regime, but mainly as a social process. Producing a categorization or taxonomy of the Commons by a type of resource can be misleading, as Bollier (2014) warns us:

> While choosing to categorize commons by the type of resource involved is tempting, a focus on the resource alone can be misleading. For example, a 'knowledge commons' on the Internet is not simply about intangible resources such as software code or digital files; such a commons also requires physical resources to function (computers, electricity, food for human beings). By the same token, 'natural resource commons' are not just about timber or fish or corn, because these resources, like all commons, can only be managed through social relationships and shared knowledge.

In other words, to quote Helfrich (2013), 'all commons are social, and all commons are knowledge commons'. Our relationships to shared goods that are managed as Commons should be the focal point and, thus, we should discuss the process of Commoning. In other words, we should discuss the process of the circulation of the free/open/participatory: 'free' and 'open' ensure access to raw material to build the Commons; 'participatory' refers to the process of broad participation in order to actually build it. The Commons, then, becomes the institutional format used to prevent private appropriation of shared creations, and the circle is closed when Commons-generated material is once again free/open raw material for the next circulation of the Commons.

The 'Global Commons' approach (upper-right) focuses on a larger scale in relation to the resilient communities quadrant, that is, on the Commons with a global orientation (Figure 7.1). Advocates and builders of this scenario argue that the Commons should be created and fought for on a transnational global scale. Though production is distributed and therefore facilitated at the local level, the conjunction of CBPP with desktop manufacturing technologies could create sustainable business ecologies. There, the resulting micro-factories, essentially networked on a global scale, would profit from mutualized global cooperation, both on the design of the product and on the improvement of common machinery. 'Micro-factories' is a concept that refers to small dimension, automated factories capable of greatly conserving resources such as space, energy, materials and time (Tanaka, 2001; Okazaki, Mishima

DOI: 10.1057/9781137406897.0015

and Ashida, 2004). They are likely to feature automatic machine tools, assembly systems, evaluation and control systems, a quality inspection system and waste elimination system (Kussul et al., 2002; Koch, 2010). For example, see the Wikispeed's project micro-factory in Seattle, which is a licensed light-industrial space the size of a shipping container, used as a prototyping facility for cars that can get more than 100 miles per gallon (Denning, 2012). The Wikispeed car is produced voluntarily by a network of developers from all over the world, who have managed to significantly reduce the development time and cost compared with conventional car manufacturing, through the use of methods similar to those of CBPP (Dafermos, 2014; Denning, 2012). The Wikispeed project was launched in the 2008 Progressive Insurance Automotive X-PRIZE competition for the development of energy-efficient cars (Dafermos, 2014). The resolution to apply CBPP development methods to car manufacturing was what separated this project from its competition (ibid.). When the founder of this project, Joe Justice, posted his plans on the Web, volunteers gathered and shortly after, a functioning prototype was presented (Denning, 2012; Halverson, 2011). More than 150 volunteers contribute now, and their goal is to deliver Wikispeed as a complete car for $17,995 and as a kit for $10,000 (Wikispeed, 2012). To sum up, as Dafermos (2014) puts it, Wikispeed, just like that of Open Source Ecology and RepRap projects, demonstrates how a technology project can leverage the open design Commons and P2P infrastructures to engage the global community in its development. Most importantly, Wikispeed suggests a model of distributed manufacturing that is well-suited to a post-fossil fuel economy: a model which is small scale ('on-demand'), decentralized, energy efficient and locally controlled (Dafermos, 2014).

Any distributed enterprise, such as the ones being developed around the aforementioned projects, is seen in the context of transnational 'phyles', that is, alliances of ethical enterprises that operate in solidarity around a particular knowledge Commons (P2P Foundation, 2014; de Ugarte, 2014). As the key terrain of conflict is around the relative autonomy of the Commons vis-à-vis for-profit companies, we are in favor of a preferential choice toward entrepreneurial formats which integrate the value system of the Commons, rather than profit maximization. In that context, phyles, in other words the creation of businesses by the community, can make the Commons viable and sustainable in the long run. Advocates and builders of this scenario struggle for a shift from the current flock of community-oriented businesses toward business-enhanced

DOI: 10.1057/9781137406897.0015

communities. They believe that we need corporate entities which are sustainable from the inside out, not just via external regulation from the state, but from their own internal statutes and links to Commons-oriented value systems. We are arguably living the endgame of neoliberal material globalization based on cheap energy, which necessitates relocalization of production (see the resilient communities scenario). However, we have new possibilities for online, affinity-based socialization, coupled with the resulting physical interactions and community building. The value-creation communities of this quadrant might be locally based but are globally linked. Out of that, new forms of business organization may arise, which are substantially more community-oriented. This scenario sees no contradiction between global open design collaboration and local production: both can occur simultaneously, so the relocalized reterritorialization will be accompanied by global tribes, organized in phyles. The various Commons, based on shared knowledge, code and design, will be part of these new global knowledge networks, but closely linked to relocalized implementations.

Therefore, political and social mobilization on the regional, national and transnational scale is seen as part of the struggle for the transformation of institutions. Participating enterprises are vehicles for the commoners to sustain Global Commons as well as their own livelihoods. This scenario does not take social regression as a given and believes in sustainable abundance for the whole of humanity. It envisions a transition to a paradigm which would include new decentralized and distributed systems of provisioning and democratic governance, escaping the pathologies of the current political economy and constructing an ecologically sustainable alternative (Bollier, 2014). To achieve such a transition, the Global Commons scenario suggests that we should work on building both global and local political and social infrastructures. Next, we venture into some general transition proposals for the state and the market in order to realize the full potential of the ICT-driven TEP in a more sustainable and just way.

DOI: 10.1057/9781137406897.0015

9

Transition Proposals toward a Commons-Oriented Economy and Society

Abstract: *There is arguably a need for political and social mobilization on regional, national and transnational scale, with a political agenda that would transform people's expectations, the economy, the infrastructures and the institutions in the vein of a Commons-oriented political economy. According to Kostakis and Bauwens, the latter is not a utopia or just a project for the future. Rather it is rooted in an already existing social and economic practice. This chapter concludes with some transition proposals for moving toward a global Commons-oriented economy which can take full advantage of the current techno-economic paradigm's potential in a more sustainable and just way.*

Kostakis, Vasilis and Michel Bauwens. *Network Society and Future Scenarios for a Collaborative Economy*. Basingstoke: Palgrave Macmillan, 2014. DOI: 10.1057/9781137406897.0016.

In the midst of the current techno-economic transformations, humanity is at a crossroads. How will a degraded natural environment sustain a political economy based on the assumption that natural resources are an endless sink? How will the modern, participatory ICT be fine-tuned, with the assumption that potentially abundant cultural/knowledge resources would exist in artificial scarcity? What value models will be adopted for a deployment period to come? Which model will prevail? According to Brynjolfsson and McAfee (2011) 'When the changes happen faster than expectations and/or institutions can adjust, the transition can be cataclysmic'. To avoid such a cataclysm, we arguably need political and social mobilization on the regional, national and transnational scale, with a political agenda that would transform our expectations, our economy, our infrastructures and our institutions in the vein of a Commons-oriented political economy. The latter is not a utopia or simply a project for the future. Rather, it is rooted in an already existing social and economic practice, that of the CBPP, which is producing Commons of knowledge, code and design, and has created real economies such as the FLOSS economy, the open hardware economy and others. In its broadest interpretation, concerning all the economic activities emerging around open and shared knowledge, it has increasingly been contributing trillions of dollars to the GDP of the USA, according to the Fair Use Economy report (Rogers and Szamosszegi, 2011) (and one should reckon how difficult it is for the GDP index to consider socially produced use value).

We have already described the micro-economic structures of this emerging Commons-oriented economic model, which we can summarize as follows: at the core of this new value model are contributory communities, consisting of both paid and unpaid labor, which are creating common pools of knowledge, code and design. These contributions are enabled by collaborative infrastructures of production, and a supportive legal and institutional infrastructure, which enables and empowers the collaborative practices. These infrastructures of cooperation, that is technical, organizational and legal infrastructures, are very often enabled by democratically run foundations. These foundations are more generically called 'for-benefit associations', which may create code/design/knowledge depositories; protect against infringements of open and sharing licenses; organize fundraising drives for infrastructure; and organize knowledge sharing through local, national and international conferences. Thus, they are an enabling and protective mechanism. Finally, successful projects

DOI: 10.1057/9781137406897.0016

create an economy around the Commons pools, based on the creation of added value products and services that are based on the common pools, but also add to them. This is done by entrepreneurs and businesses that operate in the marketplace. Most often, these are for-profit enterprises, creating an 'entrepreneurial coalition' around the Commons and the community of contributors. They hire developers and designers as workers, create livelihoods for them and support the technical and organizational infrastructure, also including the funding of foundations. On the basis of this generic micro-economic experiences, it is possible to deduce adapted macro-economic structures as well, which would include a civil society that consists mainly of communities of contributors creating shareable Commons; of a new state form, which would enable and empower social production generally and create and protect the necessary civic infrastructures; and an entrepreneurial coalition which would conduct commerce and create livelihoods (Figure 9.1).

If we look at the micro-level, we recommend the intermediation of cooperative accumulation. In today's FLOSS economy we have a paradox: the more 'communist' the sharing license we use (i.e., no restrictions

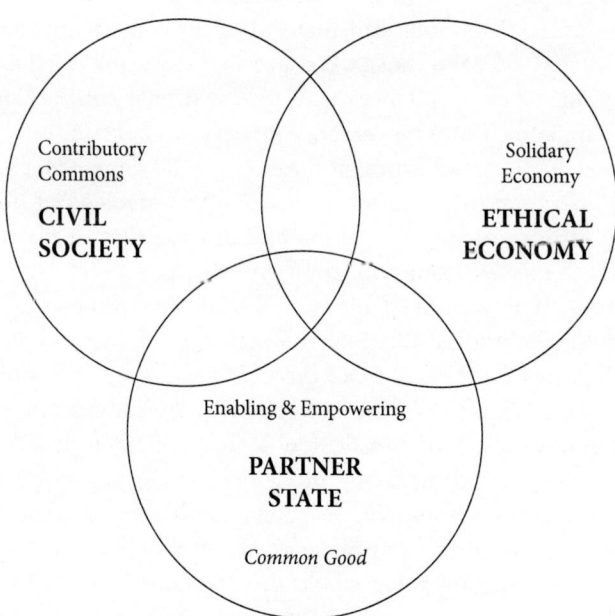

FIGURE 9.1   *The Commons-oriented economic model of mature peer production*

DOI: 10.1057/9781137406897.0016

on sharing) in the peer production of free software or open hardware, the more capitalist the practice (i.e., multinationals can use it for free). Take, for example, the Linux Commons which has become a corporate Commons as well, enriching big, for-profit corporations. It is obvious that this works in a certain way and seems acceptable to most free software developers. But is this way optimal? Indeed, the GPL and its variants allow anyone to use and modify the software code (or design), as long as the changes are integrated back in the commons pool under the same conditions for further users. Our argument does not focus on the legal, contractual basis of the GPL and similar licenses, but on the social logic that they enable, which is: it allows anybody to contribute, and it allows anybody to use. In fact, this relational dynamic is technically a form of 'communism': from each according to his/her abilities, to each according to his/her needs. This paradoxically allows multinational corporations to use free software code for profit maximization and capital accumulation. The result is that we do have an accumulation and circulation of information Commons, based on open input, participatory processes and Commons-oriented output; but it is subsumed to capital accumulation. Therefore, it is not currently possible, or at least easy, to have social reproduction (i.e., to create sustainable livelihoods) within the sphere of the Commons. The majority of the contributors participate on a voluntary basis, and those who have an income make a living either through wage labor or alliances with capital-driven entities. Hence the free software and culture movements, however important they might be as new social forces and expression of new social demands, are also, in essence, 'liberal' in the tradition of the political ideology of liberalism. We could say they are liberal-communist and communist-liberal movements, which create a 'communism of capital'.

The question is whether Commons-based peer production, that is, a new proto-mode of production, can generate the institutional capacity and alliances needed to break the political power of the old order. Ultimately, the potential of the new mode is the same as those of the previous proto-modes of production – to emancipate itself from its dependency on the old decaying mode, to become self-sustaining and thus replace the accumulation of capital with the circulation of the Commons. This would be an independent circulation of the Commons, where the common use value would directly contribute to the further strengthening of the Commons and of the commoners' own sustainability, without dependence on capital. How could this be achieved? Is there

DOI: 10.1057/9781137406897.0016

an alternative? We believe that there is: to replace the non-reciprocal licenses, that is those which do not demand a direct reciprocity from its users, with one based on reciprocity. We argue that the Peer Production License (PPL), designed and proposed by Kleiner (2010), exemplifies this line of argument. PPL should not to be confused with the Creative Commons (CC) non-commercial (NC) license, as its logic is different. The CC-NC offers protection to individuals reluctant to share, as they do not wish a commercialization of their work that would not reward them for their labor. Thus the CC-NC license stops further economic development based on this open and shared knowledge, and keeps it entirely in the not-for-profit sphere. The logic of the PPL is to allow commercialization, but on the basis of a demand for reciprocity. It is designed to enable and empower a counter-hegemonic reciprocal economy that combines a Commons that is open to all that contribute, while charging a license fee for the for-profit companies who would like to use it without contributing. Not that much changes in practice for the multinationals; they can still use the code if they contribute, as IBM does with Linux. However, those who do not contribute should pay a license fee – a practice they are used to. Its practical effect would be to somehow direct a stream of income from capital to the Commons, but its main effect would be ideological, or if you like, value-driven.

The entrepreneurial coalitions that are linked around a PPL-based Commons would be explicitly oriented toward their contributions to the Commons, and the alternative value system that it represents. From the point of view of the peer producers or commoners, a Commons-based reciprocal license, such as PPL, would allow the contributory communities to create their own cooperative entities. In this new ecology, profit would be subsumed to the social goal of sustaining the Commons and the commoners. Even the participating for-profit companies would consciously contribute under a new logic. This proposal would link the Commons to an entrepreneurial coalition of ethical market entities (co-ops and other models) and keep the surplus value entirely within the sphere of commoners/cooperators, instead of leaking out to the multinationals. In other words, through this convergence (or rather combination) of a Commons model for abundant immaterial resources, and a reciprocity-based model for the 'scarce' material resources, the issue of livelihoods and social reproduction could be solved. The surplus value would be kept inside the Commons sphere itself. The cooperatives, through their cooperative accumulation, would fund the production of

DOI: 10.1057/9781137406897.0016

immaterial Commons, because they would pay and reward the peer producers associated with them. In this way, peer production could move from a proto-mode of production, unable to perpetuate itself on its own outside capitalism, to an autonomous and real mode of production. It would create a counter-economy that could be the basis for reconstituting a 'counter-hegemony' with a for-benefit circulation of value. This process, allied to 'pro-Commons' social movements, could be the basis for the political and social transformation of the political economy. Hence we might move from a situation in which the communism of capital is dominant, to a situation in which we have a 'capital for the Commons', increasingly insuring the self-reproduction of the peer-production mode.

The new open cooperativism would be substantially different from the previous form. In the old one, internal economic democracy is accompanied by participation in market dynamics on behalf of the members, using capitalist competition. There is an unwillingness to share profits and benefits with outsiders, therefore, no creation of the Commons. We argue that an independent Commons-oriented economy would need a different model in which the cooperatives produce Commons and are statutorily oriented toward the creation of the common good. To realize their goals they should adopt multistakeholder forms of governance which would include workers, users-consumers, investors and the concerned communities. Today we have a situation where open communities of peer producers are largely oriented toward the start-up model and are subsumed to profit maximization, while the cooperatives remain closed, use exclusive intellectual property licenses, and, thus, do not create a Commons. In the new model of open cooperativism, a merger should occur between the open peer production of the Commons and the cooperative production of value. The new open cooperativism would (i) integrate externalities; (ii) practice economic democracy; (iii) produce Commons for the common good; (iv) and socialize its knowledge. The circulation of the Commons would be combined with the process of cooperative accumulation, on behalf of the Commons and its contributors. In the beginning, the immaterial Commons field, following the logic of free contributions and universal use for everyone who needs it, would co-exist with a cooperative model for physical production, based on reciprocity. But as the cooperative model would become more and more hyper-productive through its ability to create sustainable abundance in material goods, the two logics could merge.

DOI: 10.1057/9781137406897.0016

It is important to highlight that the Commons-based reciprocal licenses, such as PPL, are not merely about redistribution of value, but about changing the mode of production. Our approach is to transform really existing peer production, which today is not a full mode of production, being incapable of assuring its own self-reproduction. This is exactly why the convergence of peer production in the sphere of abundance must be linked to the sphere of cooperative production, to ensure its self-reproduction. As with past phase transitions, the existence of a proto-counter-economy and the resources that this allocates to the counter-hegemonic forces are absolutely essential for political and social change. This was arguably the weakness of classic socialism, in that it had no alternative mode of production and could only institute state control after a takeover of power. In other words, it is difficult, if not impossible, to wait and see the organic and emergent development of peer production into a fully alternative system. If we follow such an approach, peer production would just remain a parasitic modality dependent on self-reproduction through capital. We argue that the expectation that one can change society merely by producing open code and design, while remaining subservient to capital, is a dangerous pipe dream. Through the ethical economy surrounding the Commons, by contrast, it becomes possible to create non-commodified production and exchange. We thus envision a resource-based economy which would utilize stigmergic mutual coordination through the gradual application of open book accounting and open supply chain. We believe that there will be no qualitative phase transition merely through emergence, but that it will require the reconstitution of powerful political and social movements which aim to become a democratic polis. And that democratic polis could indeed, through democratic decisions, accelerate the transition. It could take measures that obligate private economic forces to include externalities, thereby ending infinite capital accumulation.

However, such changes at the level of the micro-economy might not survive a hostile capitalist market and state without necessary changes at the macro-economic level (Kostakis and Stavroulakis, 2013). We should not ignore the fact that the state has its own interests in perpetuating its bureaucracy and legitimacy. Gajewska (2014) emphasizes this argument through the case of the campus food services (free lunches) at Concordia University as an example of peer production in the physical world. She describes the tension between the university administration and the P2P food services collectives which were producing food Commons. The

DOI: 10.1057/9781137406897.0016

project started with 'direct action' occupying university space for cooking, eventually recognized by Concordia University. What we realize is that a transition narrative should take into account the possibility for creating spaces of democratic accountability from below. For example, in the aforementioned case, the university was the framework through which students could pool resources in the form of fee levies and organize for-benefit projects (Gajewska, 2014). Hence, there is a need for transition proposals carried by a resurgent social movement that embraces new value creation through the Commons, and becomes the popular and political expression of the emerging social class of peer producers and commoners. This movement should arguably be allied with the forces representing both waged and cooperative labor, independent Commons-friendly entrepreneurs and agricultural and service workers.

To begin with, we introduce the concept of the Partner State Approach (PSA), in which the state becomes a 'partner state' and enables autonomous social production. The PSA could be considered a cluster of policies and ideas whose fundamental mission is to empower direct social-value creation, and to focus on the protection of the Commons sphere as well as on the promotion of sustainable models of entrepreneurship and participatory politics. It is important to emphasize that we consider the 'partner state' as the ideal condition for a government to pursue (as is the case in Ecuador with the FLOK society project) and the P2P movement to fight for. While people continue to enrich and expand the Commons, building an alternative political economy within the capitalist one, by adopting a PSA the state becomes an arbiter, retreating from the binary state/privatization dilemma to the triarchical choice of an optimal mix among government regulation, private-market freedom and autonomous civil-society projects. Thus, the role of the state evolves from the post-World War II welfare-state model, which could arguably be considered a historical compromise between social movements for human emancipation and capitalist interests, to the partner state one, which embraces win-win sustainable models for both civil society and market. In such an approach, the state would strive to maximize openness and transparency while it would systematize participation, deliberation and real-time consultation with the citizens. Thus, the social logic would move from ownership-centric to citizen-centric. The state should de-bureaucratize through the commonification of public services and public-Commons partnerships. Public service jobs could be considered a common pool resource, and participation could be extended to the

DOI: 10.1057/9781137406897.0016

whole population. Furthermore, representative democracy would be extended through participatory mechanisms (participatory legislation, participatory budgeting etc.). It would also be extended through online and offline deliberation mechanisms as well as through liquid voting (real-time democratic consultations and procedures, coupled with proxy voting mechanisms). In addition to this, taxation of productive labor, entrepreneurship and ethical investing, as well as taxation of the production of social and environmental goods should be minimized. However, taxation of speculative unproductive investments, taxation on unproductive rental income and taxation of negative social and environmental externalities should be augmented. In these ways, the partner state would sustain civic Commons-oriented infrastructures and ethical Commons-oriented market players, reforming the traditional corporate sector in order to minimize social and environmental externalities. Last but not least, of great importance would be the engagement of the partner state in debt-free public monetary creation while supporting a structure of specialized complementary currencies.

The second component of a Commons-oriented economy would be an ethical market economy, that is, the creation of a Commons-oriented social/ethical/civic/solidarity economy. Ethical market players would coalesce around the Commons of productive knowledge, eventually using peer production and Commons-oriented licenses to support the social-economic sector. They should integrate common good concerns and user-driven as well as worker-driven multistakeholders in their governance models. Ethical market players would move from extractive to generative forms of ownership, while open, Commons-oriented ethical company formats are privileged. They should create a territorial and sectoral network of 'chamber of Commons' associations to define their common needs and goals and interface with civil society, commoners and the partner state. With the help from the partner state, ethical market players would create support structures for open commercialization, which would maintain and sustain the Commons. Ethical market players should interconnect with global productive Commons communities (i.e., open design communities) and with global productive associations (phyles) which project ethical market power on a global scale. We suggest that ethical market players should adopt a 1–8 wage differential and minimum and maximum wage levels. The mainstream commercial sector should be reformed to minimize negative social and environmental externalities, while incentives which aim for a convergence between

DOI: 10.1057/9781137406897.0016

the corporate and solidarity economy must be provided. Hybrid economic forms, such as fair trade and social entrepreneurship, could be encouraged to obtain such convergence. Distributed micro-factories for (g)localized manufacturing on demand should be created and supported in order to satisfy local needs for basic goods and machinery. Institutes for the support of productive knowledge should also be created on a territorial and sectoral basis. Education should be aligned with the co-creation of productive knowledge in support of the social economy and the open Commons of productive knowledge. Therefore, all publicly funded research and innovation should be released under the GPL (for an extensive discussion of this proposal, see Boldrin and Levine's (2013) as well as Pearce (2012)). Additionally, Commons infrastructures for both immaterial and material goods have to be created: in such a political economy, society is seen as a series of interlocking Commons supported by an ethical market economy and a partner state that protects the common good and creates supportive civic infrastructures. Local and sectoral Commons would create civil alliances of the Commons to interface with the chamber of the Commons and the partner state. Interlocking for-benefit associations (knowledge Commons foundations) would enable and protect the various Commons. In addition to this, solidarity cooperatives should form public-Commons partnerships in alliance with the partner state, while the ethical economy sector could be represented by the chamber of Commons. Also, the natural Commons should be managed by a public-Commons partnership and based on civic membership in Commons trusts.

We would like to stress that this list of transitional strategies and preliminary proposals for policymaking is general and non-inclusive. By no means does this chapter intend to formulate a specific economic plan or a clearly defined transitional policy to a Commons-based society. It is important to remember Bouckaert and Mikeladze's (2008, p. 7) advice that 'a more sophisticated diagnosis, as a function of culture, context, and systems features' allows for 'selective transfers, for inspiration by other good practices, for adjustments of solutions, for facilitated learning by doing, for trajectories which are fit for purpose'. Hence, a fundamental belief on which this book is premised is the fact that there are no universal 'how-to' manuals, because not only does every nation have its own special characteristics, but also rapid social change based on grandiose systemic substitutions usually has disastrous results, as history shows; many times these results are contradictory

DOI: 10.1057/9781137406897.0016

to what ambitious but benevolent revolutionaries may struggle for. Therefore, this chapter is an attempt to introduce suggestions and ideas for a post-capitalist society and draw attention to the promising, creative rhetoric of a PSA for Commons-oriented development. We might argue that four factors in a certain state could catalyze the transition toward a Commons-based society: (i) the extended micro-ownership of fixed capital such as land, machinery and so on; (ii) the need for recomposing the productive infrastructures, as is the case in defaulted states; (iii) an already existent robust network of solidarity and cooperative initiatives; (iv) a decentralized energy network. Further interdisciplinary research around these newly developed concepts and ideas on a global basis is imperative, along with initiating a debate between scholars and activists in order to fine-tune the transition scenarios toward Commons-oriented economies and societies.

DOI: 10.1057/9781137406897.0016

Conclusions

Kostakis, Vasilis and Michel Bauwens. *Network Society and Future Scenarios for a Collaborative Economy*. Basingstoke: Palgrave Macmillan, 2014. DOI: 10.1057/9781137406897.0017.

▶

DOI: 10.1057/9781137406897.0017

We discussed three models of value creation, redistribution and economic development:

▸ The classical proprietary capitalism, currently in decline.
▸ The mixed model of cognitive capitalism which is manifested by two different technological regimes/future scenarios. Netarchical and distributed capitalism are aimed at capital accumulation either for the benefit of global shareholders (NC), or for networks of for-profit enterprises and individuals (DC). However, in NC the design of the infrastructure (the back-end) is in the hands of centralized privately owned platforms, whereas in DC the infrastructure is primarily distributed with the promise to make everyone a small capitalist.
▸ The hypothetical mature peer production model whose seeds can be found not only in the global Commons (GC) scenario, but also in the resilient communities (RC) one. They are aimed at improving the circulation of the Commons for the local community (RC) and the transnational Commons (GC). In both scenarios the control is distributed through free self-allocation by the commoners. In the RC the commoners affect the governance and design of their infrastructures on a local scale, whereas in the GC approach the commoners try to build global infrastructures.

Under the conditions of traditional proprietary capitalism we have seen that workers create value in their private capacity as providers of labor. In addition, managerial and engineering layers are introduced in order to manage collective production on behalf of the capitalist owners. The codified knowledge is proprietary and the value is captured as IP rent. The owners of capital capture and realize the market value, whereas there is partial redistribution for the workers in the form of wages. Under conditions of capital-labor balance, the state redistributes wealth to the workers as consumers. However, under the contemporary conditions of labor weakness, the state redistributes wealth to the financial sector and creates conditions of debt dependence for the majority of the population. This value model is becoming obsolete because it contradicts the essential characteristics of the ICT-driven TEP, but is also based on a profoundly counterproductive, twofold logic of social organization. On the one side, this logic stems from a false concept of abundance in the limited material world, since it has created a system based on infinite growth within the confines of finite resources. On the other, it promotes a false concept of scarcity in the infinite immaterial world and instead of allowing continuous experimental social innovation, it purposely erects legal and technical barriers to prevent free cooperation through strict copyright, patents and so on. Therefore, the first priority for a sustainable civilization should be transforming these principles into their opposites. We argued that the rise of peer production signals new alternative paths for the deployment of the current TEP. This proto-mode of production is both immanent and transcendent vis-à-vis capitalism, because it has features that strongly decommodify both labor and immaterial value and institute a field of action based on P2P dynamics and a P2P value system. Peer production functions not only within the cycle of accumulation of capital but also within the new cycle of creation and accumulation of the Commons.

The key idea of this book is to distinguish the condition of the P2P/ Commons/sharing practices under the dominance of financialized cognitive capitalism, and a more genuine civil/ethical model centered on the Commons. Under conditions of emerging peer production while financial capitalism is still dominant, we saw that civic voluntary contributors, paid labor and independent entrepreneurs create value codified in common pools of knowledge, code and design. The capital owners realize and capture the market value of both contributors and labor, while the proprietary network platforms capture and realize the attention value of the sharers/contributors. The capital owners also profit from the benefits of disaggregated distributed labor (i.e., crowdsourcing). The Commons are managed by for-benefit institutions which reflect the balance of influence between contributors, labor and capital owners, but continue to expand the common pools. However, the Commons sector lacks solidarity mechanisms to cope with precarity and, thus, civil society is still derivate to the market and state sectors. The state weakens its public service and solidarity functions, in favor of its repressive functions as well as subsidizing financial capital. It barely contributes to the co-creation of the conditions for peer production whereas redistribution to financial capital continues.

Under conditions of strong, mature peer production through civic dominance, that is 'genuine' CBPP, we saw that civic voluntary contributors and autonomous cooperative labor would create codified value through common pools. Labor and civic re-skilling could occur through Commons-oriented distributed manufacturing, which places value creators at the helm of distributed manufacturing and other forms of value

DOI: 10.1057/9781137406897.0017

creation. Commons contributors should create cooperative Commons-oriented market entities that sustain the Commons and their communities of contributors. Hence, cooperative and other Commons-friendly market entities would not only co-create common pools but also engage in cooperative accumulation on behalf of their members. Therefore, Commons-oriented contributions should be codified in their legal and governance structures while entrepreneurial coalitions and phyles are formed, meaning structured networks of firms working around joint common pools to sustain Commons-producing communities. Furthermore, the Commons-enabling for-benefit institutions would become a core civic form for the governance of common pools, while the associated market entities would create solidarity mechanisms and income for the peer producers and commoners, supported by the partner state. The state, dominated by the civic/Commons sectors, becomes a partner state which creates and sustains the civic infrastructure necessary to enable and empower autonomous social production. The market becomes a moral and ethical economy, oriented around Commons production and mutual coordination supported by the partner state functions. The market sector is dominated by cooperative, Commons-oriented legal, governance and ownership models, while the remaining profit-maximizing entities are reformed to respect environmental and social externalities.

The hypothetical model of mature peer production can arguably be considered a working alternative which can perform better than the current dominant value model while solving a number of systemic problems. We have attempted to highlight the existence of creative communities who are building the political economy they desire within the confines of the political economy they mean to transcend. Peer production, then, should be seen as a social advancement within capitalism but with various post-capitalistic aspects in need of protection, enforcement, stimulation and connection with progressive social movements. In the midst of a turning point, it is high time we supported a sustainable alternative capable of breaking the shackles of capitalist opportunism and ushering in a new political economy based on the finer aspects of the human spirit. It is high time the accumulation of capital was replaced by a full circulation of the Commons.

DOI: 10.1057/9781137406897.0017

References

Anderson, C. (2012) *Makers: The New Industrial Revolution* (London: Random House).

Aoki, K. (2009) 'Free Seeds, Not Free Beer: Participatory Plant Breeding, OpenSource Seeds, and Acknowledging User Innovation in Agriculture', *Fordham Law Review, 77*(5), 2275–2310.

Arvidsson, A., and Pietersen, N. (2013) *The Ethical Economy: Rebuilding Value after the Crisis* (New York, NY: Columbia University Press).

Baran, P. A., and Sweezy, P. M. (1966) *Monopoly Capital: An Essay on the American Economic and Social Order* (New York, NY: Monthly Review Press).

Barnes, P. (2006) *Capitalism 3.0: A Guide to Reclaiming the Commons* (San Francisco, CA: Berrett-Koehler Publishers).

Bauwens, M. (2005) 'The Political Economy of Peer Production', *CTheory Journal*, http://www.ctheory.net/articles.aspx?id=499, date accessed 11 April 2014.

Bauwens, M. (2009) 'Class and Capital in Peer Production', *Capital & Class, 33*, 121–141.

Bell, D. (1973) *The Coming of Post-Industrial Society* (New York, NY: Basic Books).

Benkler, Y. (2006) *The Wealth of Networks: How Social Production Transforms Markets and Freedom* (New Haven, CT: Yale University Press).

Benkler, Y. (2011) *The Penguin and the Leviathan: The Triumph of Cooperation over Self-Interest* (New York, NY: Crown Business).

DOI: 10.1057/9781137406897.0018

Bessen, J., and Meuer, M. (2009) *How Judges, Bureaucrats, and Lawyers Put Innovators at Risk* (Princeton, NJ: Princeton University Press).

Boldrin, M., and Levine, D. (2007) *Against Intellectual Monopoly* (New York, NY: Cambridge University Press).

Boldrin, Michele, and David K. Levine (2013) 'The Case against Patents', *Journal of Economic Perspectives*, 27(1): 3–22.

Bollier, D. (2002) 'Reclaiming the Commons: Why We Need to Protect Our Public Resources from Private Encroachment', *Boston Review*, 27, 3–4.

Bollier, D. (2005) *Brand Name Bullies: The Quest to Own and Control Culture* (Hoboken, NJ: Wiley).

Bollier, D. (2009) *Viral Spiral: How the Commoners Built a Digital Republic of Their Own* (New York, NY: New Press).

Bollier, D. (2014) 'The Commons as a Template for Transformation', *Great Transition Initiative*, http://www.greattransition.org/document/ the-commons-as-a-template-for-transformation, date accessed 11 April 2014.

Bollier, D., and Helfrich, S. (2012) *The Wealth of Commons* (Amherst, MA: Levellers Press).

Bouckaert, G., and Mikeladze, M. (2008) 'Introduction', *The NISPAee Journal of Public Administration and Policy*, 1(2), 7–8.

Boutang, Y. M. (2012) *Cognitive capitalism* (Cambridge: Polity Press).

Boyle, J. (2003a) 'Foreword: The Opposite of Property?' *Law and Contemporary Problems*, 66, 1–32.

Boyle, J. (2003b) 'The Second Enclosure Movement and the Construction of the Public Domain', *Law and Contemporary Problems*, 66, 33–74.

Brown, M. T. (2010) *Civilizing the Economy: A New Economics of Provision* (Cambridge: Cambridge University Press).

Brynjolfsson, E., and McAfee, A. (2011) *Race against the Machine: How the Digital Revolution Is Accelerating Innovation, Driving Productivity, and Irreversibly Transforming Employment and the Economy* (Lexington, MA: Digital Frontier Press).

Bulajewski, M. (2012) 'An Ambitious Plan For Putting Kickstarter Out of Business', *A Blog of Philosophical Reflections & Speculations*, http:// www.mrteacup.org/post/an-ambitious-plan-for-putting-kickstarter-out-of-business.html, date accessed 11 April 2014.

DOI: 10.1057/9781137406897.0018

Carpenter, S. R., Walker, B. H., Anderies, J. M., and Abel, N. (2001) 'From Metaphor to Measurement: Resilience of What to What?' *Ecosystems*, 4, 765–781.

Carson, K. (2010) *The Homebrew Industrial Revolution: A Low-Overhead Manifesto* (Charleston, SC: BookSurge Publishing).

Castells, M. (2000) *The Rise of the Network Society* (Oxford: Blackwell).

Castells, M. (2003) *The Power of Identity* (Oxford: Blackwell).

Castells, M. (2009) *Communication Power* (Oxford: Oxford University Press).

Chamberlin, S. (2009) *The Transition Timeline: For a Local, Resilient Future* (Cambridge: Green Books).

Chomsky, N. (2011) *Profit over People: Neoliberalism and Global Order* (New York, NY: Seven Stories Press).

Ciffolilli, A. (2004) 'The Economics of Open Source Hijacking and the Declining Quality of Digital Information Resources: A Case for Copyleft', *First Monday*, 9, http://www.firstmonday.org/ojs/index.php/fm/article/view/1173/1093, date accessed 11 April 2014.

Coleman, B., and Hill, M. (2004) 'How Free Became Open and Everything Else under the Sun', *M/C Journal: A Journal of Media and Culture*, 7, http://journal.media-culture.org.au/0406/02_Coleman-Hill.php, date accessed 11 April 2014.

Dafermos, G. (2012) *Governance Structures of Free/Open Source Software Development* (Delft: Next Generation Infrastructures Foundation).

Dafermos, G. (2014) Policy Paper on Distributed Manufacturing, *FLOK Society Project, Draft policy document*, http://en.wiki.floksociety.org/w/Commons-oriented_Productive_Capacities, date accessed 11 April 2014.

Dafermos, G., and Söderberg, J. (2009) 'The Hacker Movement as a Continuation of Labour Struggle', *Capital & Class*, 33, 53–73.

Davies, K. (2013) The Monster Machines Mining Bitcoins in Cyberspace That Could Make Techies a Small Fortune (But Cost $160,000 a Day to Power), http://www.dailymail.co.uk/news/article-2309673/Techies-building-powerful-computers-Bitcoins-new-digital-currency-make-millions.html, date accessed 11 April 2014.

de Ugarte, D. (2014) Trilogía de las Redes, http://lasindias.com/de-las-naciones-a-las-redes, date accessed 11 April 2014.

Denning, S. (2012) 'How Agile Can Transform Manufacturing: The Case of Wikispeed', *Strategy & Leadership*, 40(6), 22–28.

DOI: 10.1057/9781137406897.0018

Drechsler, W., Backhaus, J., Burlamaqui, L., Chang, H.-J., Kalvet, T., Kattel, R., Kregel, J., and Reinert, E. (2006) 'Creative Destruction Management in Central and Eastern Europe: Meeting the Challenges of the Techno-Economic Paradigm Shift' in T. Kalvet & R. Kattel (eds.) *Creative Destruction Management: Meeting the Challenges of the Techno-Economic Paradigm Shift* (Tallinn: Praxis Center for Policy Studies).

Drucker, P. (1969) *The Age of Discontinuity* (London: Heinemann).

Elliott, M. (2006) 'Stigmergic Collaboration: The Evolution of Group Work', *M/C Journal: A Journal of Media and Culture, 9*(2).

Eltantawy, N., and Wiest, J. B. (2011) 'The Arab Spring| Social Media in the Egyptian Revolution: Reconsidering Resource Mobilization Theory', *International Journal of Communication, 5,* http://ijoc.org/index.php/ijoc/article/view/1242/597, date accessed 11 April 2014.

Federici, S., and Caffentzis, G. (2007) 'Notes on the Edu-Factory and Cognitive Capitalism', *The Commoner, 12,* 63–70.

Folke, C. (2006) 'Resilience: The Emergence of a Perspective for Social–Ecological Systems Analyses', *Global Environmental Change, 16,* 253–267.

Foster, J. B. (2011) 'Capitalism and Degrowth: An Impossibility Theorem', *Monthly Review, 62*(8), https://monthlyreview.org/2011/01/01/capitalism-and-degrowth-an-impossibility-theorem, date accessed 11 April 2014.

Freeman, C. (1974) *The Economics of Industrial Innovation* (Harmondsworth: Penguin Books).

Freeman, C. (1996) *The Long Wave in the World Economy* (Aldershot: Edward Elgar).

Fuchs, C., Schafranek, M., Hakken, D., and Breen, M. (2010) 'Capitalist Crisis, Communication, and Culture – Introduction to the Special Issue of TripleC', *TripleC, 8*(2), 193–204.

Fukuyama, F. (1992) *The End of History and the Last Man* (New York, NY: Free Press).

Funnell, W., Jupe, R. E., and Andrew, J. (2009) *In Government We Trust: Market Failure and the Delusions of Privatisation* (London: Pluto Press).

Gajewska, K. (2014) 'Peer Production and Prosummerism as a Model for the Future Organization of General Interest Services Provision in Developed Countries: Examples of Food Services Collectives', *World Future Review,* http://wfr.sagepub.com/content/early/2014/03/07/1946 756714522983.abstract, date accessed 11 April 2014.

DOI: 10.1057/9781137406897.0018

Galbraith, J. K. (1993) *A Short History of Financial Euphoria* (New York, NY: Whittle Books).

Giseburt, R. (2012) 'Is One of Our Open Source Heroes Going Closed Source?' *Make*, http://blog.makezine.com/2012/09/19/is-one-of-our-open-source-heroes-going-closed-source/, date accessed 11 April 2014.

Godet, M. (2000) 'The Art of Scenarios and Strategic Planning: Tools and Pitfalls', *Technological Forecasting and Social Change, 65*(1), 3–22.

Gore, A. (2013) *The Future: Six Drivers of Global Change Hardcover* (New York, NY: Random House).

Halverson, M. (2011) 'Wikispeed's 100 Mile Per Gallon Car', *Seattle Met*, http://www.seattlemet.com/issues/archives/articles/wikispeeds-100-mpg-car-january-2011/1, date accessed 11 April 2014.

Hardin, G. (1968) 'The Tragedy of the Commons', *Science, 162*, 1243–1248.

Hardt, M., and Negri, A. (2011) *Commonwealth* (Cambridge, MA: The Belknap Press).

Harvey, D. (2007) *The Limits to Capital* (London: Verso).

Harvey, D. (2010) *The Enigma of Capital: And the Crises of Capitalism* (New York, NY: Oxford University Press).

Harvey, D. (2012) *Rebel Cities: From the Right to the City to the Urban Revolution* (London: Verso).

Helfrich, S. (2013) 'Economics and the Commons? Towards a Commons-Creating Peer Economy', Economics and the Commons Conference, Berlin, http://commonsandeconomics.org/2013/06/09/silke-helfrichs-opening-keynote-towards-a-commons-creating-peer-economy, date accessed 11 April 2014.

Hertel, G., Niedner, S., and Herrmann, S. (2003) 'Motivation of Software Developers in Open Source Projects: An Internet-Based Survey of Contributors to the Linux Kernel', *Research Policy, 32*, 1159–1177.

Hess, D. (2005) 'Technology- and Product-Oriented Movements: Approximating Social Movement Studies and Science and Technology Studies', *Science, Technology, & Human Values, 4*, 515–535.

Hopkins, R. (2008) *The Transition Handbook: From Oil Dependency to Local Resilience* (Cambridge: Green Books).

Hopkins, R. (2011) *The Transition Companion: Making Your Community More Resilient in Uncertain Times* (Cambridge: Green Books).

Howe, J. (2008) *Crowdsourcing: Why the Power of the Crowd Is Driving the Future of Business* (New York, NY: Crown Business).

DOI: 10.1057/9781137406897.0018

Hyde, L. (2010) *Common as Air: Revolution, Art, and Ownership* (New York, NY: Farrar, Straus and Giroux).

IBM (International Business Machines Corporation) (2010) 'IBM Is Committed to Linux and Open Source', *IBM*, http://www-03.ibm.com/linux/, date accessed 11 April 2014.

Kalvet, T., and Kattel, R. (2006) *Creative Destruction Management: Meeting the Challenges of the Techno-Economic Paradigm Shift* (Tallinn: Praxis Center for Policy Studies).

Keen, A. (2007) *The Cult of the Amateur* (New York, NY: Doubleday).

Kelly, R., Sirr, L., and Ratcliffe, J. (2004) 'Futures Thinking to Achieve Sustainable Development at Local Level', *Foresight, 6*(2), 80–90.

Khamis, S., and Vaughn, K. (2011) Cyberactivism in the Egyptian Revolution: How Civic Engagement and Citizen Journalism Tilted the Balance, *Arab Media and Society*, 14, http://www.arabmediasociety.com/?article=769, date accessed 11 April 2014.

Kickstarter (2014) Most Funded Open Source Projects, https://www.kickstarter.com/discover/advanced?tag_id=20&sort=most_funded, date accessed 11 April 2014.

Kleiner, D. (2010) *The Telekommunist Manifesto* (Amsterdam: Institute of Network Cultures).

Kloppenburg, J. (2010) 'Impeding Dispossession, Enabling Repossession: Biological Open Source and the Recovery of Seed Sovereignty', *Journal of Agrarian Change, 10*(3), 367–388.

Koch, M. D. (2010) 'Utilizing Emergent Web-Based Software Tools as an Effective Method for Increasing Collaboration and Knowledge Sharing in Collocated Student Design Teams', *Oregon State University*, (MSc Thesis), http://ir.library.oregonstate.edu/xmlui/handle/1957/16855, date accessed 11 April 2014.

Kondratieff, N. D. (1979) 'The Long Waves in Economic Life', *Review*, 2, 519–562.

Kostakis, V. (2010) 'Peer Governance and Wikipedia: Identifying and Understanding the Problems of Wikipedia's Governance', *First Monday*, 15, http://firstmonday.org/ojs/index.php/fm/article/view/2613, date accessed 11 April 2014.

Kostakis, V. (2012) 'The Political Economy of Information Production in the Social Web: Chances for Reflection on Our Institutional Design', *Contemporary Social Science, 7*, 305–319.

DOI: 10.1057/9781137406897.0018

Kostakis, V., and Stavroulakis, S. (2013) 'The Parody of the Commons', *TripleC*, 11(2), 412–424.

Kostakis, V., Fountouklis, M., and Drechsler, W. (2013) 'Peer Production and Desktop Manufacturing: The Case of the Helix_T Wind Turbine Project', *Science, Technology & Human Values*, 38(6), 773–800.

Kussul, E., Baidyk, T., Ruiz-Huerta, L., Caballero-Ruiz, A., Velasco, G., and Kasatkina, L. (2002) 'Development of Micromachine Tool Prototypes for Microfactories', *Journal of Micromechanics and Microengineering*, 12(6), 795–812.

Lakhani, K., and Wolf, R. (2005) 'Why Hackers Do What They Do: Understanding Motivation and Effort in Free/Open Source Software Projects' in J. Feller, B. Fitzgerald, S. Hissam & K. Lakhani (eds.) *Perspectives on Free and Open Source Software* (pp. 3–22) (Cambridge, MA: MIT Press).

Lanier, J. (2010) *You Are Not a Gadget: A Manifesto* (New York, NY: Knopf).

Latouche, S. (2009) *Farewell to Growth* (Cambridge, MA: Polity).

Leigh, A. (2003) 'Thinking Ahead: Strategic Foresight and Government', *Australian Journal of Public Administration*, 62(2), 3–10.

Lessig, L. (2004) *Free Culture: How Big Media Uses Technology and the Law to Lock Down Culture and Control Creativity* (New York, NY: Penguin Press).

Lessig, L. (2006) *Code Version 2.0* (New York, NY: Basic Books).

Lewis, M., and Conaty, P. (2012) *The Resilience Imperative: Cooperative Transitions to a Steady-State Economy* (Gabriola Island: New Society Publishers).

MacCormack, A., Rusnak, J., and Baldwin, C. Y. (2007) 'The Impact of Component Modularity on Design Evolution: Evidence from the Software Industry', *Harvard Business School Technology & Operations Mgt. Unit*, 08–038, http://ssrn.com/abstract=1071720, date accessed 11 April 2014.

MacKinnon, R. (2012) *Consent of the Networked* (New York, NY: Basic Books).

Marsh, L., and Onof, C. (2007) 'Stigmergic Epistemology, Stigmergic Cognition', *Cognitive Systems Research*, 9(1–2), 136–149.

Marx, K. (1979) *A Contribution to the Critique of Political Economy* (New York, NY: Intl Pub).

Marx, K. (1992/1885) *Capital: Critique of Political Economy* (London: Penguin Classics).

Marx, K. (1993/1973) *Grundrisse: Foundations of the Critique of Political Economy* (London: Penguin).

McCann, A. (2012) 'Opportunities of Resistance: Irish Traditional Music and the Irish Music Rights Organisation 1995–2000', *Popular Music and Society*, 35(5), 651–681.

Meadows, D. (2008) *Thinking in Systems: A Primer* (Vermont, VT: Chelsea Green Publishing).

Miles, I. (2004) 'Scenario Planning' in UNIDO (ed.) *Foresight Methodologies: Training Module 2*. (Vol. 159, pp. 67–91) (Vienna: UNIDO).

Moglen, E. (2004) 'Freeing the Mind: Free Software and the Death of Proprietary Culture', *Maine Law Review*, 56(1), 1–12.

Mollison, B. (1988) *Permaculture: A Designers' Manual* (Tyalgum: Tagari Publications).

Moore, P., and Karatzogianni, A. (2009) 'Parallel Visions of Peer Production', *Capital & Class*, 33, 7–11.

Morozov, E. (2012) *The Net Delusion: The Dark Side of Internet Freedom* (New York, NY: Public Affairs).

Mueller, M. L. (2010) *Networks and States: The Global Politics of Internet Governance* (Cambridge, MA: MIT Press).

Mulgan, G. (2013) *The Locust and the Bee: Predators and Creators in Capitalism's Future* (Princeton, NJ: Princeton University Press).

Nakamoto, S. (2008) Bitcoin: A Peer-to-Peer Electronic Cash System, http://bitcoin.org/bitcoin.pdf, date accessed 11 April 2014.

Neeson, J. M. (1993) *Commoners: Common Right, Enclosure and Social Change in England, 1700–1820* (Cambridge: Cambridge University Press).

O'Neil, M. (2009) *Cyberchiefs: Autonomy and Authority in Online Tribes* (London: Pluto Press).

O'Mahony, S. (2003) 'Guarding the Commons: How Community Managed Software Projects Protect Their Work', *Research Policy*, 32(1179–1198).

Okazaki, Y., Mishima, N., and Ashida, K. (2004) 'Microfactory – Concept, History, and Developments', *Journal of Manufacturing Science and Engineering*, 126(4), 837–844.

Orsi, C. (2009) 'Knowledge-Based Society, Peer Production and the Common Good', *Capital & Class*, 33, 31–51.

Ostrom, E. (1990) *Governing the Commons: The Evolution of Institutions for Collective Action* (Cambridge: Cambridge University Press).

DOI: 10.1057/9781137406897.0018

P2P Foundation (2014) Phyles, http://p2pfoundation.net/Phyles, date accessed 11 April 2014.

Papadopoulos, D., Stephenson, N., and Tsianos, V. (2008) *Escape Routes: Control and Subversion in the 21st Century* (London: Pluto Press).

Pariser, E. (2011) *The Filter Bubble* (New York, NY: Penguin Viking).

Patry, W. (2009) *Moral Panics and the Copyright War* (New York, NY: Oxford University Press).

Pearce, J. M. (2012) 'Physics: Make Nanotechnology Research Open-Source', *Nature, 491*, 519–521.

Perez, C. (1983) 'Structural Change and Assimilation of New Technologies in the Economic and Social Systems', *Futures, 15*, 357–375.

Perez, C. (1985) 'Long Waves and Changes in Socio-Economic Organizations', *IDS Bulletin, 16*(1), 36–39.

Perez, C. (1988) 'New Technologies and Development' in C. Freeman & B.-A. Lundvall (eds.) *Small Countries Facing the Technological Revolution* (pp. 85–97)(London: Pinter).

Perez, C. (2002) *Technological Revolutions and Financial Capital: The Dynamics of Bubbles and Golden Ages* (Cheltenham: Edward Elgar Pub).

Perez, C. (2009a) 'The Double Bubble at the Turn of the Century: Technological Roots and Structural Implications', *Cambridge Journal of Economics, 34*, 779–805.

Perez, C. (2009b) 'Technological Revolutions and Techno-Economic Paradigms', *Cambridge Journal of Economics, 33*, 185–202.

Polanyi, K. (1944/2001) *The Great Transformation: The Political and Economic Origins of Our Time* (Boston, MA: Beacon Press).

Raidu, D. V., and Ramanjaneyulu, G. (2008) 'Community Managed Sustainable Agriculture' in B. Venkateswarlu, S. S. Balloli & Y. S. Ramakrishna (eds.) *Organic Farming in Rainfed Agriculture: Opportunities and Constraints* (Hyderabad: Central Research Institute for Dryland Agriculture.).

Rifkin, J. (2011) *The Third Industrial Revolution: How Lateral Power Is Transforming Energy, the Economy, and the World* (New York, NY: Palgrave Macmillan).

Rifkin, J. (2014) *The Zero Marginal Cost Society: The Internet of Things, the Collaborative Commons, and the Eclipse of Capitalism* (New York, NY: Palgrave Macmillan).

Robb, J. (2009) 'Transition Towns and Participatory Problem Solving', *Global Guerrillas*, http://globalguerrillas.typepad.com/

globalguerrillas/2009/04/rc-journal-transition-towns-as-a-means-to-participative-problem-solving.html, date accessed 11 April 2014.

Rogers, T., and Szamosszegi, A. (2011) 'Fair Use in the U.S. Economy: Economic Contribution of Industries Relying on Fair Use', *OER Knowledge Cloud*, https://oerknowledgecloud.org/?q=content/fair-use-us-economy-economic-contribution-industries-relying-fair-use-0, date accessed 11 April 2014.

Schmidt, E., and Cohen, J. (2013) *The New Digital Age : Reshaping the Future of People, Nations and Business* (New York, NY: Alfred A. Knopf).

Schmoller, G. (1898/1893) 'Die Volkswirtschaft, die Volkswirtschaftslehre und Ihre Methode' in G. Schmoller (ed.) *Über einige grundfragen der socialpolitik und der volkswirtschaftslehre* (Berlin: Duncker and Humblot).

Scholz, T. (2012) *Digital Labor: The Internet as Playground and Factory* (New York, NY: Routledge).

Schulak, E. M., and Unterköfler, H. (2011) *The Austrian School of Economics: A History of Its Ideas, Ambassadors, & Institutions* (Auburn, AL: Ludwig von Mises Institute).

Schumpeter, J. (1975/1942) *Capitalism, Socialism and Democracy* (London: Harper and Row).

Schumpeter, J. (1982/1939) *Business Cycles* (Philadelphia, PA: Porcupine Press).

Schwartz, P. (1996) *The Art of the Long View: Planning for Future in an Uncertain World* (New York, NY: Currency Doubleday).

Sharzer, G. (2012) *No Local: Why Small-Scale Alternatives Won't Change the World* (Winchester: John Hunt Publishing).

Siefkes, C. (2012) 'The Boom of Commons-Based Peer Production' in D. Bollier & S. Helfrich (eds.) *The Wealth of Commons* (Amherst, MA: Levellers Press).

Stadler, F. (2014) *Digital Solidarity* (Lüneburg: Mute & PML Books).

Stiglitz, J. (2010) *Freefall: America, Free Markets, and the Sinking of the World Economy* (New York, NY: W.W. Norton).

Stringham, E. (2007) *Anarchy and the Law: The Political Economy of Choice* (Oakland, CA: Independent Institute).

Tanaka, M. (2001) 'Development of Desktop Machining Microfactory', *Riken Review, 34*, http://pdf.aminer.org/000/353/685/development_of_a_micro_transfer_arm_for_a_microfactory.pdf, date accessed 11 April 2014.

DOI: 10.1057/9781137406897.0018

Tapscott, D., and Williams, A. (2006) *Wikinomics: How Mass Collaboration Changes Everything* (New York, NY: Portfolio).

The Ecologist (1994) 'Whose Common Future: Reclaiming the Commons', *Environment and Urbanization*, 6(1), 106–130.

Tocqueville, A. de. (2010) *Democracy in America* (New York, NY: Signet Classics).

Torvalds, L. (1999) 'The Linux Edge' in C. DiBona, S. Ockman & M. Stone (eds.) *Open Sources: Voices from the Open Source Revolution* (pp. 101–109) (Sebastopol, CA: O'Reilly).

van der Heijden, K. (2005) *Scenarios: The Art of Strategic Conversation* (New York, NY: John Wiley & Sons).

van der Heijden, K., Bradfield, R., Burt, G., Cairns, G., and Wright, G. (2002) *The Sixth Sense: Accelerating Organisational Learning with Scenarios* (New York, NY: John Wiley & Sons).

van Wendel de Joode, R. (2005) 'Understanding Open Source Communities: An Organizational Perspective', *Delft University of Technology* (PhD Dissertation), http://repository.tudelft.nl/view/ir/uuid:297bc2ff-956b-436b-addb-98eb1d4a3b4f/, date accessed 11 April 2014.

Vargas, J. A. (2012) 'How an Egyptian Revolution Began on Facebook', *The New York Times*, http://www.nytimes.com/2012/02/19/books/review/how-an-egyptian-revolution-began-on-facebook.html?pagewanted=all&_r=1&, date accessed 11 April 2014.

Varoufakis, Y. (2013) Bitcoin and the Dangerous Fantasy of 'Apolitical' Money, http://yanisvaroufakis.eu/2013/04/22/bitcoin-and-the-dangerous-fantasy-of-apolitical-money/, date accessed 11 April 2014.

von Hippel, E., and von Krogh, G. (2003) 'Open Source Software and the Private-Collective Innovation Model: Issues for Organization Science', *Organization Science, 14*, 209–223.

Walker, B. H., and Salt, D. (2006) *Resilience Thinking: Sustaining Ecosystems and People in a Changing World* (Washington, DC: Island Press).

Walker, B. H., Abel, N., Anderies, J. M., and Ryan, P. (2009) 'Resilience, Adaptability, and Transformability in the Goulburn-Broken Catchment, Australia', *Ecology and Society, 14*(1), 12.

Webster, F. (2006) *Theories of the Information Society* (New York, NY: Routledge).

DOI: 10.1057/9781137406897.0018

Wikispeed (2012) WIKISPEED, First Car-Maker in the World to Accept Bitcoin, http://wikispecd.org/2012/07/wikispeed-first-car-maker-in-the-world-to-accept-bitcoin-press-release/, date accessed 11 April 2014.

Wilding, N. (2011) *Exploring Community Resilience in Times of Rapid Change* (Dunfermline: Fiery Spirits Community of Practice).

Wolff, R. (2010) The Keynesian Revival: A Marxian Critique, http://rdwolff.com/content/keynesian-revival-marxian-critique, date accessed 11 April 2014.

Zittrain, J. (2008) *The Future of the Internet: And How to Stop It* (New Haven, CT: Yale University Press).

Žižek, S. (2010) *Living in the End Times* (London: Verso).

DOI: 10.1057/9781137406897.0018

Index

DOI: 10.1057/9781137406897.0019

DOI: 10.1057/9781137406897.0019